The Complete Guide to Labrador Retrievers

Jo de Klerk

LP Media Inc. Publishing

Text copyright © 2020 by LP Media Inc.

All rights reserved.

No part of this book may be reproduced or transmitted in any form or by any means, electronic or mechanical, including photocopying, recording, or by an information storage and retrieval system - except by a reviewer who may quote brief passages in a review to be printed in a magazine or newspaper - without permission in writing from the publisher. For information address LP Media Inc. Publishing, 3178 253rd Ave. NW, Isanti, MN 55040

www.lpmedia.org

Publication Data

Jo de Klerk

The Complete Guide to Labrador Retrievers ---- First edition.

Summary: "Successfully raising a Labrador Retriever from puppy to old age" --- Provided by publisher.

ISBN: 978-1-952069-13-0

[1.Labrador Retrievers --- Non-Fiction] I. Title.

This book has been written with the published intent to provide accurate and authoritative information in regard to the subject matter included. While every reasonable precaution has been taken in preparation of this book the author and publisher expressly disclaim responsibility for any errors, omissions, or adverse effects arising from the use or application of the information contained inside. The techniques and suggestions are to be used at the reader's discretion and are not to be considered a substitute for professional veterinary care. If you suspect a medical problem with your dog, consult your veterinarian.

Design by Sorin Rădulescu

First paperback edition, 2020

TABLE OF CONTENTS

ACKNOWLEDGMENTS 9

CHAPTER 1
Breed Overview 10
About the Breed 11
Looks 13
Age Expectancy 14
Personality 15
Inside the Home 16
Outside the Home 17
Costs of Keeping a Labrador Retriever 19

CHAPTER 2
Breed History 22
Origin of the Breed 22
Genetics 24
Historical Standards 26
Famous Labrador Retrievers in History 27
    Breed Ambassadors: 27
    Stars of Film and Literature: 29
    Companions to the Stars 29
    Service Dogs and Heroes 30

CHAPTER 3
Behavior 32
Temperament 32
Exercise Requirements 35
Importance of Socialization 36
Trainability 37
Separation Anxiety 39
Chewing 40
Hyperactivity 42

CHAPTER 4
How to Choose a Labrador Retriever **44**
Purchasing or Rescuing? 45
Researching the Establishment 47
Inquire about the Parents 49
Looking at the Puppy 52
Considerations of a Rescue Dog 54

CHAPTER 5
Preparations for a New Dog **56**
Preparing Your Home 57
Shopping List 60
    Crates 60
    Beds 61
    Collars, Harnesses and Leashes 63
    Bowls 63
Introducing Your New Labrador Retriever to Other Dogs 65
Introducing Your New Labrador Retriever to Children 67

CHAPTER 6
Training **68**
Potty Training 70
How to Teach Sit 73
How to Teach Stay 75
How to Teach Lie Down 76
How to Teach Walk On the Leash 76
How to Teach Walk Off the Leash 77
Agility and Flyball 79

CHAPTER 7
Traveling **80**
Preparations for Travel 81
Traveling in a Car 83
Traveling by Plane 87
Vacation Lodging 87
Leaving Your Labrador Retriever at Home 88

CHAPTER 8
Nutrition **90**
Importance of Nutrition 91
Commercial Food 92

Pet Food Labels ... **93**
BARF and Homemade Diets ... **96**
Weight Monitoring ... **98**
Food Supplements ... **99**

CHAPTER 9
Dental Care ... 100
Importance of Dental Care ... 100
Dental Anatomy ... 101
Tartar Build-Up and Gingivitis ... 102
Epulis ... 102
Dental Care ... 103
Dental Procedures ... 105

CHAPTER 10
Grooming ... 106
About the Coat ... 107
Coat Health ... 108
 108
Nail Clipping ... 110
Ear Cleaning ... 111
Anal Glands ... 112

CHAPTER 11
Preventative Veterinary Medicine ... 114
Choosing a Veterinarian ... 115
Vaccinations ... 117
Microchipping ... 119
External Parasites ... 119
Internal Parasites ... 121
Neutering ... 121
Pet Insurance ... 122

CHAPTER 12
Labrador Retriever Health Conditions ... 124
Cardiac Conditions ... 124
   Atrioventricular Block ... 124
   Pericardial Effusion ... 125
   Tricuspid Valve Dysplasia ... 125
Dermatological Conditions ... 126
   Atopic Dermatitis ... 126

Endocrine Conditions ... 127
    Diabetes Mellitus ... 127
    Hypothyroidism ... 128
Digestive Conditions ... 128
    Portosystemic Shunt ... 129
Orthopedic Conditions ... 130
    Cruciate Ligament Injury ... 130
    Joint Dysplasia, Osteochondrosis and Osteoarthritis ... 131
    Limber Tail ... 132
    Panosteitis ... 133
Cancers ... 134
    Hemangiosarcoma ... 134
    Lipoma ... 135
    Mast Cell Tumor ... 135
    Osteosarcoma ... 135
Neurological Conditions ... 136
    Epilepsy ... 136
Ocular Conditions ... 137
    Cataracts ... 137
    Progressive Retinal Atrophy ... 137
Urinary Conditions ... 138
    Ectopic Ureters ... 138
Respiratory Conditions ... 138
    Laryngeal Paralysis ... 139

CHAPTER 13
Working
... 140
Field Work ... 141
Assistance Dogs for the Disabled ... 144
Search and Rescue ... 146
Police and Armed Forces Dogs ... 147

CHAPTER 14
Breeding
... 148
Deciding about Breeding ... 148
Mating ... 149
Pregnancy ... 150
Birthing ... 151
Aftercare ... 152
Raising Puppies ... 153

CHAPTER 15
Showing **156**
Selecting a Dog for Showing 156
Breed Standards 160
After Selecting Your Puppy 167
Preparing for a Show 168

CHAPTER 16
Living with a Senior Dog **170**
Diet 171
Senior Wellness Checks 172
Advanced Arthritis 173
Dementia 174
Organ Deterioration 175
Loss of Senses 176
Bladder Control 177
Saying Goodbye 178

ACKNOWLEDGMENTS

To all the Labrador owners: I wouldn't be doing what I do if it wasn't for you! In my clinical line of work, I have a particular interest in pain management. When I first graduated, again and again I saw old, creaky Labradors come into my consulting room, and I was frustrated that the pain relief I was offering them simply wasn't enough. This is what pushed me to study companion animal pain relief as a postgraduate study, as well as learn how to do Western Acupuncture. The bulk of my cases are still made up of old arthritic dogs, many of which are Labradors, and therefore it's a breed which has become close to my heart.

I would also like to thank my long-time editor, Clare Hardy. She's worked with me in the background of many of these books, and her input is absolutely invaluable. Thank you for all the hard work and effort you put into helping me turn these books into what they are! I couldn't have done it without you!

CHAPTER 1
Breed Overview

It's definitely not hard to see why the Labrador Retriever is the world's favorite dog! Nearly every positive quality you can imagine in a breed seems to come naturally to the Labrador Retriever. Labs are intelligent, trainable, full of boundless enthusiasm, and above all friendly towards humans both young and old. Although Labs were bred originally as working dogs, it wasn't long before the breed found its place in the home, as a loyal and lovable part of the family.

If you are thinking of welcoming a Labrador Retriever into your home, this book will take you through all the basics of understanding the breed and ensuring you know how to meet your dog's needs.

Photo Courtesy of Christianna Legner

CHAPTER 1 Breed Overview

Photo Courtesy of Michael Waters

About the Breed

"A Labrador Retriever should be active (but not hyper), easy to train, and should get along with adults, kids, and other dogs. They should love water and retrieving. And they should have the hallmark head of the breed with a kindly, melting expression."

Tiffany Ginkel
Cedar Ranch Labrador Retrievers

Anyone who has gotten to know a Labrador Retriever will vouch for the fact that if there is water about, they will find it. That is because the breed was originally created as a working dog to retrieve fish for fishermen in the Canadian province of Newfoundland. With their water-repellent coat and webbed paws, Labrador Retrievers thrived in their semi-aquatic roles. Highly intelligent, eager, and strong, Labradors quickly became a favorite breed of working dog for field huntsmen too. But it is the lovable personality and gentle nature of the breed that makes Labradors such perfect family dogs, and probably the most adaptable of all breeds as human helpmates and companions.

Photo Courtesy of Geoffrey Rhoades

CHAPTER 1   Breed Overview

Looks

The Labrador Retriever is a glossy, short-haired dog of medium to large size, and comes in three colors: black, yellow, and chocolate.

The original Labradors were almost always black. Black is the dominant gene over the yellow and chocolate colors, which are sometimes termed golden and liver. In the early years, yellow and chocolate were seen as "off colors" and were bred out, or sometimes culled. Today, all three colors are equally recognized by the Kennel Club, although in the field, the black Labrador is more commonly seen. Today's Labs are usually a single solid color, though in the early years of the breed, they sometimes had white paws and a white muzzle, the areas that tend to gray in elderly Labs.

The Labrador Retriever may appear to be a large breed, as a healthy dog is sturdy and well-muscled, but they are classified as medium-large, standing up to 24" at the withers. Females are slightly smaller than males. The AKC standard's ideal weight for males is 65–80 lb (29–36 kg) and for females is 55–70 lb (25–32 kg). The Labrador has a notoriously voracious appetite, and is prone to putting on weight, especially if a dog doesn't get enough exercise, so the owner of a Labrador should always be especially careful not to let their dog become obese, which can lead to many health problems.

The Labrador's water-repellent coat is certainly an asset, as however much attracted he is to mud and water, his coat is easily hosed or brushed off and requires only minimal grooming. However, the Lab does molt twice a year in the spring and fall, and will shed quite profusely all year round. This is because the Lab has a double-coat, meaning he has an insulated undercoat to protect him from the cold, which is great for his comfort in the outdoors, but not so great for your furniture! It also means a Labrador may not suit you if you have allergies in the family. Brushing your dog outdoors every day will help to ensure he brings as little as possible of his loose hair indoors.

Of course, full credit to the Labrador's good looks can't be done without reference to his sunny personality, which shines in his lively brown eyes and characteristic smile. With attributes like these, it is easy to forgive a bit of hair on the carpet!

Age Expectancy

The lifespan of a Labrador Retriever is 10-14 years, with an average of around 12 years. Chocolate Labradors tend to have a slightly shorter lifespan of around 10 years. Studies* suggest that this is because the chocolate gene is recessive, meaning both parents need to be carriers in order to produce chocolate pups. This has resulted in a smaller gene pool, and with less genetic diversity comes a greater tendency to genetic diseases. Although the yellow gene is also recessive, the greater popularity of this color has expanded the gene pool, so they are less affected. But as with any pedigree dog, for the greatest chance of a long, healthy life, you should look for parents with pedigrees that show as little inbreeding as possible.

If you are buying a Labrador as a puppy, you need to consider any changes that may occur in your personal circumstances over his projected lifespan, and whether you can commit to your dog's care for the whole of his life.

*[*McGreevy, P.D., Wilson, B.J., Mansfield, C.S. et al. Labrador retrievers under primary veterinary care in the UK: demography, mortality and disorders. Canine Genet Epidemiol 5, 8 (2018).]*

Photo Courtesy of Jillian Torres

CHAPTER 1   Breed Overview

Personality

> *"Labs are also very people centric and do not make good 'yard' dogs (left in the outdoors by themselves). They need to be part of your family and day to day life."*
>
> ***Neil and Jodi Martin***
> *Carriage Hill Labradors*

The Labrador Retriever is an enthusiastic dog, with the drive to work hard, and the intelligence to adapt willingly to any demand. Labs are eager to please and follow your instructions, and it makes living with a Labrador Retriever greatly rewarding, as the love you lavish on your pet is returned in full, with unswerving loyalty and devotion. The Labrador's natural trainability makes him an excellent working dog, as well as an easygoing member of the family. To get the most out of your best friend, however, it's important to train him.

Chapter 3 of this book goes into more detail about the behavior of a Labrador Retriever. It notes that although there is an accepted standard personality for the breed, there will be variations for many reasons. In the case of the Labrador, many people claim that personality differences exist between the three colors. For example, the black Labrador, seen so widely in the field, is thought of as a driven and patient hunter. The yellow Lab is seen as a sweet-natured family dog, and the chocolate Lab is thought to have a more independent streak. In actual fact, the color gene in itself is irrelevant to the Labrador's personality, but breeding for specific traits can produce a variation. So, where the black Lab has been preferred as a working dog, it has been selected and bred for its active and focused qualities. And as the yellow Lab became a family favorite, this color variant was selectively bred for its quieter, friendly nature.

The other circumstance that may affect the personality of a Labrador is sadly man-made. If you are adopting an older dog from a rescue, his early experiences may have damaged his trust and made him unnaturally fearful, and in rare cases even aggressive. Or he may simply never have been trained to meet his potential. So, there will be work to do with a rescue dog, to forge a bond and bring out his true personality. As an intelligent and friendly breed, however, there is always a good chance of rehabilitating a Labrador and giving him a fresh start.

A Labrador Retriever will fill your home with joy and entertainment. Your Lab is the one friend you will never have to second-guess, as his honest and unconditional love puts everything into perspective at the end of the day.

Inside the Home

Photo Courtesy of Tanya De La Garza

The Labrador Retriever is a medium-large dog and with his exuberant nature, he will fill a space both physically and metaphorically! The Lab is not ideally suited to apartment living as he needs both indoor and outdoor space. If your Lab has no other option but to live in an apartment, because he is an assistance dog, for example, then he will have had special training to cope with it, but he will still need plenty of exercise for his physical and mental wellbeing.

If you are buying a puppy, bear in mind how large your Labrador will become when he is fully grown. If you are new to the breed, it may be worth inviting a friend to your house who has an adult Labrador or similar sized dog, to get a feel for the effect such a large dog will have on your personal space. If you are living alone and this is unlikely to change, you may find there is plenty of room for you and a lively Labrador in a modestly sized home. If you have a large family however, you need to think about the space your Labrador will occupy and its effect on the children's play space, the living area, and workspace of other adults in the home. Of course, your dog does not necessarily have to have access to the whole house, as long as the rooms in which he is allowed are large enough and free from hazards. This is a matter of individual preference, but should be carefully considered before committing to sharing your home and the next 12 years of your life with a large, energetic dog.

As previously mentioned, although the Labrador Retriever has a short coat, it does shed, so you should be prepared for hair and dander in the house. Dander is tiny flecks of skin that all animals shed, and is particularly allergenic. There are many vacuum cleaners on the market specifically designed for homes with pets. They have extra suction and HEPA filters to help keep your house hair and allergen-free, and are well worth the investment. Hard floors are an advantage over carpets as they are easily cleaned, do not harbor fleas, and do not soak up the inevitable potty-training accidents. If you have carpets, you may wish to consider a carpet shampooing machine. Leather furniture is easily wiped down and does not attract hair like textile coverings.

Unfortunately, a Labrador will not suit some people, since its dander and shedding undercoat can provoke a reaction in severe allergy sufferers.

CHAPTER 1   Breed Overview

You may also wish to consider whether any regular visitors to your home, such as extended family, are allergic to dogs before settling on a Labrador Retriever. As the Labrador is the most popular breed of service dog, it has been crossed with the Poodle, which has a non-shedding coat, to produce the Labradoodle for those with allergies who require a service dog. However, the Labradoodle is by no means guaranteed to be hypoallergenic, and can be less reliable than a Labrador.

There's no getting away from it, the Labrador Retriever is known to be on the smellier end of the doggy-odor spectrum. This is on account of his thick double coat, that hangs on to natural doggy odors. But many people have no objection to the Labrador's signature smell, and can even find it quite endearing. In the home, you will probably become nose-blind to it quite quickly, even if your visitors don't. On the other hand, many Labradors love to roll in anything unsavory they find outdoors, which can bring some very pungent odors into your home. Other odors you should be prepared for include gas, which is usually due to an inappropriate diet, anal glands, which may sometimes get clogged and release a foul discharge, and potty-training accidents. If you are particularly sensitive to less than fragrant odors in the home, the Labrador may not be the dog for you!

If you have considered the impact of having a Labrador share your house, and decide that all the positive benefits your four-legged friend will bring will more than make up for the small sacrifices, then there's no doubt that a Lab in the family will make your house into a home!

Outside the Home

A Labrador Retriever ideally requires that you have your own back yard. If you do not have a private yard, you will need access to a safe space immediately outside your home for toileting, and extra walks during the day to make up for the absence of a yard. A fully fenced, secure back yard is preferable because you can make it a relaxing outside space, where your dog can be off-leash and enjoy the fresh air.

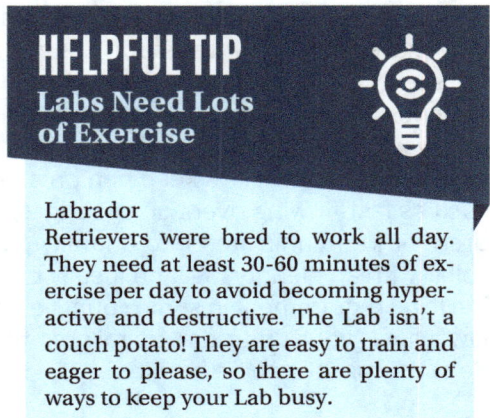

HELPFUL TIP
Labs Need Lots of Exercise

Labrador Retrievers were bred to work all day. They need at least 30-60 minutes of exercise per day to avoid becoming hyperactive and destructive. The Lab isn't a couch potato! They are easy to train and eager to please, so there are plenty of ways to keep your Lab busy.

Labradors are an athletic breed, so you should ensure that your yard fence is high enough to prevent him from jumping out, ideally at least 6 feet high with no gaps. It should also go right to the ground if you have a puppy who could squeeze underneath. Also, if you have a Labrador that digs, you should supervise him outside, in case he tunnels under the fence. Divert your dog's digging instinct by providing a sand pit with buried treats, so that he has a permitted area to exercise his instincts and leaves your flower beds alone!

If you are adopting a dog from a shelter, you will likely have a home check, regardless of whether or not you have had dogs before. If you are new to dog ownership, the home check is an ideal opportunity to have an experienced eye cast over your outdoor space. The home checker will make suggestions if they see any broken fence panels, other escape routes or hazardous objects. This doesn't mean your application will be refused, but you will need to correct these problems before you can bring your rescue dog home.

If you are buying a puppy and have never had a dog before, you probably won't have a home check, although some breeders may check out their puppies' new homes. If not, you could ask an experienced dog owning friend to check your yard for reassurance that you haven't overlooked anything. Further advice on how to prepare your home and garden is found in Chapter 5.

The Labrador Retriever was bred to work outdoors, and has high exercise needs, so your dog also needs access to open spaces where he can run and explore. To enable him to safely enjoy this freedom, it is important that he is trained to have good recall. Training is discussed in detail in Chapter 6.

Dogs love their familiar walks just as much as the joy of discovering new places, and your Labrador will get great pleasure in checking out all the scents around his wider territory. Your dog's physical and mental health depends on him getting out, especially if you live somewhere without your own yard. You should take sensible precautions for the safety of your dog in public spaces. Always keep him on a leash near traffic, and danger spots such as fast-flowing rivers or cliff edges, or where he might intimidate children, or jump uninvited into a family picnic. Your dog should also wear a collar with an identity tag, and ideally be implanted with a microchip, which is a legal requirement in some countries. Make sure the microchip company always has your up-to-date details, so that in the unfortunate case of your dog straying, he can be reunited.

CHAPTER 1   Breed Overview

Costs of Keeping a Labrador Retriever

The first cost involved when acquiring a Labrador Retriever is the price of the dog, and as a Lab is a pedigree breed, this will be relatively high. On average you may expect to pay $500-$2,000 for a Labrador Retriever with a registered pedigree. While you may pick up a dog for a lower price, you need to be aware that a dog without papers may be the result of casual or inexperienced breeding, or a money-making operation that ignores the dogs' welfare. So, a "cheap" Labrador puppy is likely to have more health issues further down the line. Alternatively, if you are taking on a rescue dog from a shelter, these dogs are not free. You will always need to pay a rehoming fee. This may be in the region of $200-$500 and goes to cover the general costs the rescue incurs in their work, such as neutering, vaccinations, microchipping, fostering, accommodations, feeding, transport and administration. And it ensures no one uses a rescue as a place to pick up a free dog for illegal dog fighting, breeding or reselling.

Labrador Retrievers are quite costly dogs to keep due to their size and potential health issues. Preventative veterinary medicine is discussed in Chapter 11, and insurance for veterinary fees is strongly recommended from the outset, especially for a Labrador. Alternatively, some owners prefer to put aside a regular amount for unforeseen veterinary costs. If this is your choice you should be aware that veterinary costs for a Labrador can run into thousands of dollars, and to find yourself short of life-saving funds at a critical moment could force you to make very hard decisions. You will also have other regular costs such as parasite treatments and annual vaccinations which should figure in the budget. Some vets do monthly plans to help budget regular health costs for your dog.

On a day-to-day basis, the cost of feeding your Labrador Retriever will be higher than average, because he is large and energetic. Also, because the breed is predisposed to joint issues and other health problems in later life, you need to ensure he is on a high-quality diet. Nutrition is discussed in Chapter 8, and once you have an idea which type of food you want for your dog, it is worth calculating how much you would be feeding an adult Labrador according to the manufacturer's guidelines, to arrive at a monthly cost. Don't forget your dog deserves a treat from time to time, especially during his training, so build a little into the budget for this as well.

If your Lab is your first dog, you will need to invest in some equipment up front. And as your dog outgrows, wears out or destroys his bedding, crate, harness, toys, leashes etc., you will need to replace them as you go along. Chapter 5 will discuss things you need to have on hand for your new dog.

Jo de KLERK | The Complete Guide to Labrador Retrievers

Photo Courtesy of Debbie Wilson

CHAPTER 1   Breed Overview

Owning a Labrador opens up a world of optional activities. Many are free of charge, and others require class fees, entry fees, equipment or other services. Dog training is the first activity that every new owner needs to put in place. If you have owned dogs before, you may already be confident that you can train your dog yourself, and some tips are given in Chapter 6. On-line videos are also an excellent training resource. However, joining training classes provides plenty of camaraderie and support, as well as the valuable opportunity to socialize your dog. There will usually be a fee, but it is well worth it. Likewise, other activities that your Lab may enjoy, such as Agility classes and Flyball sessions, will involve a fee and possibly some additional equipment. If you plan to compete at a higher level there will also be additional costs. And if you wish to show your dog, you will need to be prepared for entry fees, travel costs and all the expenses involved in keeping your dog in tiptop cosmetic condition. These are discussed in Chapter 15.

So, although keeping a Labrador Retriever is more costly than the average dog, a lot of the expenses are optional, and you can keep the costs down. The choice of a Labrador Retriever doesn't mean you have to be wealthy, as long as present and future expenses have been budgeted for. All that matters to your easygoing Labrador is that he is comfortable, adequately fed, well exercised, free from pain and has human company for a good portion of the day, with the opportunity to meet other dogs as well. If you can guarantee him these basic requirements, then you have a friend for life!

CHAPTER 2
Breed History

Origin of the Breed

Labrador is a region in Canada, and it would stand to reason that the Labrador Retriever originated here. However, to be more specific, the earliest of the Labrador's grandparents originated in Newfoundland as long ago as the 1500s. But there was already a distinct breed called the Newfoundland, that was larger than the Labrador, with a higher tail carriage. So, in the early days, the Labrador became known as the St. John's Dog or Lesser Newfoundland, and was the result of crossing the Newfoundland with small water dogs to create a nimble working dog for Canadian fishermen. Just like the breed we know today, the early Labradors had webbed toes and a water-repellent coat. And their thick tapering tail (known as an otter tail) served as a powerful rudder. So, they were in their element in cold water, retrieving fish that had fallen from the hooks or bringing in the nets.

Photo Courtesy of Lisa Higbee

CHAPTER 2   Breed History

The St. John's Dogs were seen as workaholics that thrived on their job, and would work enthusiastically beyond the point of exhaustion. But they also found a place in the family, when fishermen would bring them home to play with the children, so the hallmarks of a truly all-around dog were evident in the Labrador's ancestors, even many centuries ago.

It wasn't until the 1800s that the Labrador came to wider attention, when the 2nd Earl of Malmesbury saw the breed in action in Newfoundland, and brought them home to Heron Court in Poole, England, for use in waterfowling. Other aristocratic promoters of the Labrador breed were the 10th Earl of Home and his nephews the 5th Duke of Buccleuch and Lord John Scott, who saw the potential of the Labrador as a gundog. As the nineteenth century progressed, successive family heirs continued to breed and refine the Labrador, with the name being coined by the 3rd Earl of Malmesbury in the 1880s, since Labrador and Newfoundland were seen by the British as the same land mass at this time.

Three of the 6th Duke of Buccleuch's foundation Labradors were given to him by the 3rd Earl of Malmesbury, after the Duke had been hugely impressed by the Earl's Labradors on a shooting party in Dorset. The Duke's Labrador Kennel at Langholm in the Scottish Borders, subsequently became the largest in Britain, with the best of the Malmesbury and Buccleuch bloodlines mated to produce a strong and strictly maintained pedigree, even to this day:

"The main characteristics of the traditional Buccleuch Labrador are a good nose, a tender mouth and an intelligent and courageous temperament. Their heads are often shorter than the average Labrador; they have a thick double coat and frequently have the 'otter' tail. The pure strain can only throw black puppies."

[Source: www.drumlanrigcastle.co.uk]

In 1903, the Labrador was recognized by the English Kennel Club, and in 1917, the American Kennel Club followed suit in registering its first Labrador Retriever.

Back in the UK, the Buccleuch Kennel suffered a downturn in the first half of the twentieth century, for various reasons including the war years. However, the breeding program was reestablished in the post-war years, and across continents, the Labrador Retriever worked its way to the top of Kennel Club registrations, becoming the officially recognized favorite breed in many countries.

Genetics

The genetics of the Labrador Retriever is most evident in its three distinct colors, black, yellow and chocolate. To arrive at their coloring, every Labrador Retriever carries a combination of four main genes. These genes are B and E types, and comprise a big B and a little b, and a big E and a little e. A Labrador can have these in various combinations.

The B genes are easy if you think of them as standing for Black and Brown. The big B contains an instruction to make a lot of color, giving a black coat, whereas the little b contains an instruction for less color, causing a brown coat. But big B is a dominant gene, so it will override a small b. Consequently, BB and Bb make black, and bb makes brown.

However, what about yellow Labradors? This is where the E genes come in. A Labrador will inherit a pair of these too. Big E is dominant but it doesn't affect color. However little e switches off color. So, if a Labrador inherits two little e's, he will be yellow.

There is one final set of genes, the D genes, standing for Dilute. If a Labrador inherits two recessive little d genes, it makes his coat lighter. This is how you sometimes get Labradors in charcoal, champagne and silver colors.

The Kennel Club recognizes only black, chocolate and yellow as official Labrador colors. However, sometimes shade variations occur. There is

CHAPTER 2   Breed History

Photo Courtesy of Ashleigh Greule

some controversy over why this is, with some arguing for the presence of a recessive dd gene (D standing for Dilute). However, as the Labrador is not considered to be a natural carrier of the dd gene, some claim that it is the result of cross-breeding, even decades ago. Another explanation for lighter coat colors is that the ee gene can act more like a

dimmer switch than an on-off switch. Silver and champagne Labradors are certainly beautiful, but are not generally accepted as pure breeds by the Kennel Club.

With the exception of yellow Labradors, you never know what recessive genes a Labrador is carrying, so all colors can appear in a litter. Of course, experienced breeders will have a good idea of the recessive genes in their dogs, and have a fair idea of the likely colors of their pups.

Whatever the combination of color genes passed down to your Labrador puppy, one thing is sure, he will certainly have inherited the special blend of intelligence, liveliness and affection that is the hallmark of the breed.

Historical Standards

During the early years of the breed, when the Labrador was still known as the St. John's Dog, and was working in Canadian waters, there was no breed standard as we know it today. But the dog was bred for certain practical qualities: a short, dense, waterproof coat, webbed toes, an "otter tail," and an enthusiasm for work. These are attributes we still see in today's Labradors, although our attitude to color has changed. As already noted, the early dogs were all black, with "off-colors" often euthanized. But whereas today's black, yellow, chocolate and dilute variant colors are mostly solid, the St. John's dog sometimes had a white muzzle and paws.

One of the first observations of the qualities that made the Labrador such a promising addition to the English hunting kennels was made by Colonel Peter Hawker, a celebrated diarist, author and sportsman. Colonel Hawker visited Newfoundland in 1814, and described the St. John's Dog as having an excellent sense of smell, flexibility in the field, and speed. In his account, he said of the breed that it is:

"...oftener black than of another color and scarcely bigger than a pointer. He is made rather long in head and nose; pretty deep in the chest; very fine in the legs; has short or smooth hair, does not carry his tail so much curled, and is extremely quick and active in running and swimming ... The St John's breed of these dogs is chiefly used on their native coast by fishermen. Their sense of smelling is scarcely to be credited. Their discrimination of scent ... appears al-

CHAPTER 2   Breed History

most impossible ... For finding wounded game of every description, there is not his equal in the canine race; and he is a sine qua non in the general pursuit of waterfowl."

(Source: Hawker, P. 1830, Instructions to Young Sportsmen in All that Relates to Guns and Shooting)

With qualities such as these, the two main kennels in Britain that developed the breed set about refining the breed to their own high standards, as every country gentleman's shooting companion.

It was not until the early twentieth century when the breed was recognized by the British and American Kennel Clubs, and an official breed standard drawn up, and this is discussed in greater detail in Chapter 15 on showing your dog.

Famous Labrador Retrievers in History

The Labrador Retriever is such a popular and adaptable dog that his happy face can be seen everywhere, and it's no surprise that many Labs have come to public attention. Here we recognize a few of the biggest names in the Labrador Hall of Fame:

Breed Ambassadors:

Ben of Hyde belonged to Major Radcliffe and was born in 1899. Although the Labrador breed was well established by the turn of the twentieth century, it was dominated by the popular black color, and Ben of Hyde was the first documented yellow Labrador Retriever. Ben of Hyde and his son Neptune are considered to be the source of most of the yellow Labradors today.

King Buck (1948–1962) was struck with distemper early in life, but pulled through and went on to become a Field Trials champion, with a record of success that was not matched for 40 years. He came to wider attention as the first dog to appear on a United States Fish and Wildlife Service Duck stamp (1959), which always featured a water-

> **NOT-SO-FUN FACTS**
> **Genetic Conditions**
>
> As with any breed, Labrador Retrievers are prone to many genetic problems. In addition to having one of the highest cancer rates, Labs are also prone to hip dysplasia, elbow dysplasia, epilepsy, and more. That's why it's crucial to find a breeder who does extensive genetic testing on all his or her breeding dogs.

Photo Courtesy of Abbie Alhashimi

fowl. The artwork was created by Maynard Reece, and showed King Buck carrying a mallard drake.

Nell was the Earl of Home's dog from the Buccleuch estate, and was described both as a Labrador and a St. John's dog. She was the first of the breed to be photographed, in 1856, and her photograph shows her to have a black coat, with white paws and muzzle.

Stars of Film and Literature:

Junkyard was a yellow Labrador in the Disney movie Race to Witch Mountain in 2009. He was played by Buck, whose other movie credits include Eight Below (2006), and Snow Dogs (2002).

Marley is a yellow Labrador who starred in the movie Marley & Me (2009). As Marley aged throughout the movie, he was played by different canine actors. The movie is based on the true-life story "Marley & Me: Life and Love with the World's Worst Dog" by John Grogan.

Spike was a famous yellow Labrador-Mastiff cross, from a rescue background. He was owned by Frank Weatherwax, who trained dogs for acting roles, and in 1957 he starred in the Disney movie Old Yeller. He also starred in She-Creature (1956) and The Silent Call (1961). On the small screen he featured in TV shows such as The Westerner, Hondo and The Mickey Mouse Club, and in the TV series Lassie, he starred as Barney, Chuka and Skipper. Spike's son Junior played Rontu in Island of the Blue Dolphins.

Companions to the Stars

Buddy and Seamus were the pet Labradors of former United States President Bill Clinton. Buddy was a chocolate Labrador that did not get on with the White House cat. Tragically in 2002, four-year-old Buddy was killed by a car, which Bill Clinton described as "by far, the worst thing" to happen to him since leaving office. Shortly after this, the Clintons acquired another chocolate Labrador named Seamus, who was Buddy's great-nephew from the same kennels.

Koni (1999 – 2014) was the black Labrador Retriever companion of Russian President Vladimir Putin. Her full name was Connie Paulgrave. Koni hit the headlines when President Putin brought her into a meeting with German Chancellor Angela Merkel in 2007, which did not go down well with the Chancellor, who had been left with a fear of dogs after suffering an attack in 1995.

Sully was a yellow Labrador named after the pilot that safely landed a stricken commercial aircraft on the Hudson River in 2009. Sully was a trained military service dog, and served with former US President George H.W. Bush during the last six months of his life. He rose to public attention on social media when photographed sleeping next to the president's coffin. Sully subsequently went on to serve in the rehabilitation of injured US servicemen.

Service Dogs and Heroes

Dorado was a yellow Labrador that belonged to Omar Riviera, when the pair were on an upper floor of the World Trade Center on the day of the 9/11 attack. Although Dorado's owner tried to push him to safety several times, the dog would not leave his side, and led him down 70 floors, just before the tower collapsed.

Jake the black Labrador is another hero of the 9/11 attacks. As a trained search and rescue dog, he worked a relentless 17-day stint to locate survivors and victims at the World Trade Center, burrowing tirelessly through "white-hot, smoking debris." Jake also helped search for victims of Hurri-

Photo Courtesy of Chris Norton

cane Katrina and Hurricane Rita in 2005. Jake had been abandoned as a puppy, with a broken leg and dislocated hip, but he rose to become one of fewer than 200 U.S. government-certified rescue dogs. He also worked as a therapy dog with burn victims and nursing home residents. Jake died of cancer in 2007 at the age of 12.

Lucky and Flo were two black Labradors from the same litter, trained to sniff out optical equipment such as pirated CDs and DVDs. In 2007 they became famous for sniffing out nearly 2 million unlicensed counterfeit DVDs in Malaysia for the Motion Picture Association of America. This feat led to the arrest of the software pirates, and a ten-thousand-dollar bounty put on the two dogs' heads!

Sabi, a black Labrador with a white blaze on her chest, was a member of the Australian Special Forces serving in Afghanistan. As a sniffer dog, she was trained to detect explosive devices. Sabi became separated from her handler during a battle in 2008, and subsequently went missing in action in the Afghan desert for over a year, where she was detained by Taliban fighters. She was recovered safe and well in 2009.

CHAPTER 3
Behavior

"Labs have a lot of energy, but they have a great disposition and are great with kids. They are also a very versatile breed. They've been used for hunting, agility trials, service dogs, and police/drug sniffing dogs in addition to being great family pets."

Lauren McNeely
Bayard Acres Labrador Retrievers

Temperament

One of the main reasons that the world has taken the Labrador Retriever to its heart is down to the Lab's wonderful temperament.

In a nutshell, Labrador Retrievers are usually friendly, active and outgoing. The British Kennel Club states the Labrador should be *"intelligent, keen and biddable, with a strong will to please. Kindly nature, with no trace of aggression or undue shyness."* (KC 2018). And the American Kennel Club breed standard describes the Labrador temperament as:

"The ideal disposition is one of a kindly, outgoing, tractable nature; eager to please and non-aggressive towards man or animal. The Labrador has much that appeals to people; his gentle ways, intelligence and adaptability make him an ideal dog. Aggressiveness towards humans or other animals, or any evidence of shyness in an adult should be severely penalized."

(AKC 1994)

The breed standard sets a benchmark to ensure that all registered Labrador Retrievers can be relied upon to possess the temperament that is the hallmark of the breed, and it is very rare that a Labrador is found to be aggressive or fearful, except where he has been let down by the humans in his life. Though the breed is naturally forgiving, that trust can't be rebuilt in the most severe cases. The other factor that may result in an atypical Labrador temperament, is as a result of successive ca-

CHAPTER 3 Behavior

sual breedings, where the parents have not been selected for their excellent temperaments. There may even be other breeds in the mix. By always buying from a Kennel Club Registered Breeder, you have the best chance of acquiring a Labrador whose temperament reflects the best of the breed.

Anyone taking on a Labrador Retriever should understand that in order for his temperament to shine, he needs to be given a job to do, and plenty of opportunity to use his brain and burn off his considerable energy. Any negative behavior a Labrador might develop can be a result of a lack of stimulation, so when a Lab's owner plays their part, that's when the Lab will play his, and show just why the breed is so well loved the world over.

Photo Courtesy of Tim Choldas

Photo Courtesy of Monica Hillesheim

CHAPTER 3   Behavior

Exercise Requirements

"Growth plates close on Lab puppies at 14 months of age; so no long distance running on hard surfaces until after that time. It's best to stay on soft surfaces such as grass in the early months."

Lori Lutz
Bowery Run Labradors

The very first thing anyone taking on a Labrador Retriever should consider is the exercise requirement of the breed. An adult Labrador should have at least one hour of exercise a day, with some Labs from working lines needing 1.5 to 2 hours. This can be split into two or three walks, and most of it should ideally be off-leash, so your Labrador can burn off his excess energy and explore his natural environment. This makes recall training your number one priority with a Lab, as discussed in Chapter 6.

It is especially important that Labradors get sufficient exercise, as their slow metabolism and voracious appetite means they are very prone to obesity, which puts great strain on their joints and vital organs, affecting their wellbeing and life expectancy.

The recommended one hour of exercise applies only to an adult Labrador, and when your dog reaches his senior years, he will need to slow down. Of course, he will still appreciate getting out for an hour, but the pace should be gentler, and you may find several shorter walks suit him better. Living with a senior dog is thoroughly discussed in Chapter 16.

Likewise, it is important that your Labrador puppy shouldn't go out right away for an hour of vigorous exercise, as his bones and growth plates are still underdeveloped. Undue stresses on the developing growth plates can result in a misshapen or shortened limb, which could cause permanent lameness, or problems in later life. A Labrador's growth plates are not typically set until 14 months. So, until your puppy reaches puberty, he should just go out for short, controlled walks. Some of his mental and physical exercise needs can probably be met in your back yard with things like a treat ball, walking over poles, scent tracking and puzzle toys, as well as daily obedience training. Developing puppies should not play high intensity games like fetch, or jump on and off furniture.

Importance of Socialization

"They can be exposed right away to other dogs that you know are up to date on their vaccinations. Once your pup is fully vaccinated, socialize with friendly, appropriate dogs as much as possible. However, I do not recommend dog parks, because injuries to your dog can be common by other dogs behaving badly."

Tiffany Ginkel
Cedar Ranch Labrador Retrievers

Labradors are outgoing, sociable dogs, both with humans and their own kind. So, for their own mental wellbeing, they need ample opportunity to make friends and continue the education that their mother began from the day they were born.

Although most Labradors are naturally well-adjusted dogs, problems can occur if a Lab is not allowed to socialize with other dogs and humans from an early age. So as soon as your puppy has had his first set of vaccinations, it's a great idea to find a local puppy class. You may be able to locate puppy classes in your area online, otherwise, your vet is sure to have contact details. They may even run a puppy class in the veterinary surgery. Puppy classes are a great springboard to obedience training classes, but in the early days, it's enough of an education for your dog just meeting other dogs and getting to speak his own language. Puppies interact with each other in a unique way, and if your puppy only ever meets adult dogs, he will miss out on this part of his development.

Tips for managing encounters with other dogs, and socializing your dog with children are given in Chapter 5.

"Make sure you know and trust the dogs you bring your puppy around. As the saying goes, bad company corrupts good morals. Make sure the other pets behave well and won't teach bad habits to your puppy."

Kathy Jackson
Karemy Labs

CHAPTER 3   Behavior

Trainability

"Labs are fairly easy to train as they want to please you. Be consistent in how you ask for them to do something. Training in a class setting is recommended vs. shipping the dog to a trainer as the training is as much for owner as dog. Owners need to learn how to communicate well with their dog and be consistent and clear."

Neil and Jodi Martin
Carriage Hill Labradors

The Labrador Retriever is one of the most trainable breeds in the world, which is why the Lab is the first choice for assistance and search and rescue roles. That doesn't mean a Labrador puppy pops into the world fully trained and ready to go. It just means that as the owner of a Labrador, you have the most intelligent and willing dog you could hope for, with masses of potential just waiting to be reached.

Your Labrador is smart though! If you want him to be good, you have to work with him, otherwise he will use his active mind to get into mischief. Remember, he was bred as a working dog, and even if you have no plans to work him, he still needs to be stimulated and kept mentally and physically active in order to be his best self. He also responds well to positive, firm and consistent training in order to know who is boss, even while being your best friend.

Training should start as soon as your puppy comes home, as at this age his brain is a sponge, and the work you put in from the start will shape his obedience for life. It will also ensure that as he grows, he does not become a nuisance on account of his increasing size, strength and energy. A well-trained dog is also less of a danger to himself.

Training classes are an excellent idea, even if you have trained dogs before. But with a dog as smart as a Labrador, you might progress to advanced training and activities, which will really bring out your dog's talents and be great fun for you both!

Photo Courtesy of Rebecca Cawvey

CHAPTER 3   Behavior

Separation Anxiety

The very qualities you love in your Labrador, his intelligence and his affection for you, are the qualities that can lead to separation anxiety on the inevitable occasions that you have to leave him home alone. So, in order for your dog to feel comfortable on his own, he needs to know with confidence that when you leave him, you are coming back.

The earlier you can teach your dog how to be left alone the better, as separation anxiety can become an engrained behavior and be harder to overcome later in life.

If you have a puppy and are crate training him, he should be learning to see his crate as his safe space and not a prison. The advantage of leaving your puppy alone in his crate is that puppies can be destructive, and at least you can be confident he is not destroying the house while you are not there. He may also feel less anxious in a smaller space and settle more readily. You can leave some safe toys to keep him occupied, such as an antler chew, and a Kong® stuffed with a safe filling, such as wet dog food or peanut butter (but be sure that your choice of peanut butter does not contain xylitol, which is toxic to dogs).

When you first leave your dog, you do not even need to leave the house. Just step out of the room without making a fuss and shut the door. This can be for as little as a minute. You do not want to return to your dog at the point he is whining, or that will tell him that whining brings you back, so try to anticipate a point before he starts to react. Then you can return to your dog and give him gentle praise, but again, do not make a big fuss. An overreaction tells your dog that leaving and coming back are a big deal, so you want to remain calm and act like nothing exciting or unusual is happening.

If you have missed the sweet spot, and your dog has started to whine, you will need to wait for a break in his vocalizations, so that he realizes that he gets what he wants when he is quiet, and not when he is making noise.

Keep this exercise up regularly, gradually increasing the time you leave your dog. Once you get to the point where you are leaving the house for a longer period, you can always check your dog is settling by installing a dog-cam that can be viewed on your phone. That way, you will know if you are pushing ahead too fast, or if your dog is actually quite relaxed in his own company.

If separation anxiety continues to be an issue, some dogs respond well to pharmacological products designed to reduce their stress. These include DAP products, which stands for Dog Appeasing Pheromone, and mimics the calming scent released by the dog's mother during the days after birth. DAP products come as room diffusers, sprays or a collar. Other products you might try are supplements or feed containing casein or L-tryptophan. Casein is a relaxant in the mother's milk, and L-tryptophan increases the feel-good hormone, serotonin, in the brain.

If you continue to experience problems with separation anxiety, it's worth consulting a behaviorist, as their experience may identify a successful approach to set your dog on a more settled pathway.

Chewing

"Labrador retrievers relieve their anxiety with chewing so be sure to have bully sticks, carrots, apple slices, antlers to address their need to chew."

Lori Lutz
Bowery Run Labradors

Chewing may seem like a bad behavior from the owner's point of view. After all, your precious things are getting destroyed! But it is in fact natural behavior for any dog, and especially a Labrador, because as a working breed designed to retrieve game, your dog has a natural instinct to carry things in his mouth.

Chewing is also a positive thing for a puppy whose teeth are coming through, as it eases the discomfort. Also, a puppy uses the sensations in his mouth to explore his new world. Your job is to ensure that the things your puppy chews are safe for him, as he will chew indiscriminately. Most vets will at some point have had to deal with a puppy that has chewed the batteries out of something left lying around, such as the TV remote, or swallowed something indi-

> **HELPFUL TIP**
> **Separation Anxiety**
>
> One common cause of unwanted behavior is separation anxiety. If your Lab is well-behaved when you're alone but causes chaos when you're gone, it may have separation anxiety. Most dogs can overcome separation anxiety with a few tricks and tools, although some dogs with severe separation anxiety may need medication. You may need to enlist the help of a trainer if your dog has separation anxiety.

CHAPTER 3 Behavior

Photo Courtesy of Amy Seto

gestible. Children's toys will also be fair game for your puppy. How is he to know which toys are his, and which belong to the children in the family? But children's toys may be dangerous to your dog, with plastic components that may break, cause injury, or be swallowed. You need to remove hazards from your puppy's reach, as well as anything you do not want to be damaged. Crate training your dog will help him focus his chewing on his permissible objects. You can also use a puppy pen for your dog, or a playpen for your child and their toys.

"They are very mouth oriented - as they are retrievers this is hard wired. Not something you will eliminate easily. Make sure you have items that are 'theirs' that they can have and carry/mouth. If they take something you don't want them to have, offer a trade for an object they are allowed to have and then praise them when they take the offer."

Neil and Jodi Martin
Carriage Hill Labradors

Acceptable chews for your dog to gnaw on are a deer antler or Kong®, as previously mentioned. He may also enjoy a dental chew, or a raw marrowbone. Cooked bones should never be given as they may splinter. Pet stores also sell sterilized bones filled with a tasty soft marrow, that your dog can chew safely even after he has licked out all the filling. High quality dried offal can provide a tasty treat, but rawhide is not recommended as it is chemically processed and a choking hazard.

Praise your dog for appropriate chewing, and if he chews something you should have put away, just tell him "No" firmly, and remove it, then give him something he is allowed instead.

Hyperactivity

The Labrador Retriever is bred to be highly active; therefore, anyone taking this breed on should be prepared to commit fully to their dog's daily exercise needs. The single most likely cause of a hyperactive dog is one that has not had enough opportunity to burn off excess energy or use his active brain. Physically and mentally, your Labrador needs to be worked if he is not to convert his unspent energy into frustration and become hyperactive.

In addition to exercise, obedience training carried out daily will help your Labrador focus and use his brain, so that he feels more mentally fulfilled. This is especially useful for puppies who cannot do strenuous physical exercise until their growth plates are set.

Your Labrador's bloodlines may be a factor in his hyperactivity. For example, Labradors from strong working lines will live life more intensely and have more energy to expend. The yellow Labrador is also considered a quieter dog than the black Lab. This again is just down to the yellow being a more popular family dog, and consequently bred for a more placid nature.

In rarer instances, there can be a physical cause for a dog's hyperactivity. Sometimes this is a gut imbalance, that can be corrected with probiotics. Other dogs can benefit from the addition of essential fatty acids in their diet, from high quality fish oils. Or hyperactivity may be due to a deficiency of tryptophan, which may be found in chicken and turkey. If your dog gets plenty of physical and mental exercise, and you are considering a dietary cause for his hyperactivity, you should consult your vet for a full physical examination and advice.

***

Despite the possibility of a few minor hiccups at an early stage of your Labrador's life, if you give your Lab plenty of exercise, invest in training at a young age, and provide him with a healthy lifestyle, you are likely to end up with an extremely well-behaved, kind-natured dog, as this is the natural temperament bred into the Labrador Retriever's genes.

CHAPTER 4
How to Choose a Labrador Retriever

"I think it's good for people to do their research on the breed. You hear all the time that they're great family dogs (and they are) but they are retrievers. That means they like to put things in their mouths and are very prone to swallowing things! They also chew quite a bit, and the puppy stage generally lasts a full 2-3 years."

Lauren McNeely
Bayard Acres Labrador Retrievers

Photo Courtesy of Samantha Tillery

CHAPTER 4   How to Choose a Labrador Retriever

Purchasing or Rescuing?

Once you have considered all the pros and cons of owning a Labrador Retriever, and decided that you are ready to take on the commitment, the next step is to think about whether you should buy a puppy from a breeder, or adopt an unwanted dog from a shelter.

You may already have a clear idea about which route you want to go down, and there is no wrong or right choice. Your decision should depend very much on what you plan to get out of dog ownership. For some people, it may be for their children to grow up with the companionship of a dog, or for others it may be to show or work their dog, in which case, a puppy may best suit their needs. Whereas for other people, it may be for the fulfilment of rehabilitating an unwanted dog and giving it a loving home. No one should pressure you into either approach over the other, as the main thing is that whichever route you choose, a Labrador Retriever is going to become a loved and cherished member of the family, and bring as much joy to your life as you will to his.

> **HELPFUL TIP**
> **Keeping a Lab Safe is Harder Than You Expect**
>
> Labs are eating machines and will go out of their way to eat anything they can fit in their mouths, whether it's edible or not. You should puppy-proof your home as if you will have a toddler for the next 10-12 or more years—that may include cabinet locks, putting laundry in a hamper with a lid, making sure trash cans have lids, and not leaving anything on the floor you don't want to risk being eaten. Surgery to extract foreign objects from your Lab's stomach isn't cheap!

If you aspire to show your dog at a high level, you will need to buy a puppy from a registered breeder. This is because show dogs need pedigree papers. Rescue dogs rarely come with papers. This is usually due to the circumstances under which they came into the rescue, but can also be because they came from a casual or unknown breeding background. Sometimes a papered dog will be taken in by a shelter, for example, because the previous owner passed away, or due to a relationship break-up, but usually the rescue will not pass on the pedigree papers in order to give the dog a fresh start and ensure it is not sold for profit or used for exploitative breeding. This is also why most rescues will neuter their dogs, but if you wish to show a dog with the AKC, he or she is required to be unneutered. In the UK it is possible to show a neutered dog with a special exemption certificate. If you only wish to take part in local fun shows, then you will not usually need to produce a pedigree certificate, nor will it make a difference if your dog is neutered or not.

The Labrador Retriever is a working dog, so you may be more inclined towards competing in activity trials than in the show ring. In these cases, for some activities such as Field Trials and Gundog Trials, you will need a registered pedigree and enrolment on the Breed Register for your dog, but other activities such as Working Trials, Agility and Obedience are open to all dogs, as long as they are registered on the Activity Register.

So, whereas most owners planning to compete in any discipline will usually choose to purchase a puppy, rescue dogs can still find a vocation, and several Labrador Retrievers in the "Hall of Fame" in Chapter 2 came from a rescue background.

If you are choosing a working dog, you will probably be looking at specific working bloodlines, so it may suit you best to purchase a puppy from proven working stock, and train him up for the job he is required to do. However, sometimes dogs from working bloodlines can find themselves given up because their energy levels are too much for a family home. Often these dogs have missed out on early training, but for an experienced working dog owner, a shelter may provide a Labrador Retriever with a new start more suited to its temperament and abilities.

Many people choose to rescue because of the sense of satisfaction that comes with giving an unwanted dog a home and restoring his faith in the human race. And there's no doubt that rescues are full of dogs looking for their forever home, even if pedigree dogs such as the Labrador are less represented. There will be many Labrador cross breeds in shelters, however, and some rescues just rehome specific breeds, so it is worth looking online for Labrador rescues in your area if you are hoping to find your new friend in a shelter. Rescuing can be an ideal solution for older people, as to commit for the whole 12-year lifespan of a puppy may be looking too far into an unknown future. So, adopting an older dog that may be quieter than a puppy can be the perfect solution, and the dog will have one-on-one company through its golden years.

CHAPTER 4   How to Choose a Labrador Retriever

Researching the Establishment

"Take time and do your research choosing a breeder that breeds for the traits you're looking for whether that be hunting lines, confirmation, or just a great family dog."

Lauren McNeely
Bayard Acres Labrador Retrievers

If you have decided on a Labrador puppy, the one thing that should be top of your agenda, given all the health issues to which the breed is predisposed, is to look for a reputable breeder. The first stop in your search should be the Kennel Club website for your country. Simply click on "Find A Puppy" and then enter your geographical area, and you will find all the registered breeders with litters available.

If, however, you already know about Labrador bloodlines, and maybe you wish to buy a dog that comes from the same stock as others you know and admire, then you may contact the breeder directly. But you may have to go on a wait list for a puppy, especially from the more sought-after bloodlines. This is a positive thing, as it demonstrates that the breeder is not over-breeding his dogs.

When you first phone or email a breeder, there are a few things to look out for and questions to ask, before you make an appointment to visit the puppies. Remember, a good breeder will not resent a barrage of questions, and will actually welcome your thoroughness, as it demonstrates that you are taking a responsible approach to dog ownership. Good breeders take pride in their professionalism and will be only too happy to discuss their high standards of breed welfare. They should also come across as exceptionally knowledgeable about Labradors.

Photo Courtesy of Shauna Braun

Make sure you ask the following things:
1. Can I see the puppy with its mother? (All reputable breeders will agree to this.)
2. Can I see the mother's pedigree?
3. How old is the mother?
4. How many litters has the mother had?
5. What is her temperament like?
6. Has she been screened for inherited conditions and can I see the certificates?
7. Who is the father?
8. Can I see his pedigree?
9. What is his temperament like?
10. May I contact the owner of the father (if he belongs to a different owner)?
11. Can I handle all of the puppies in the litter?
12. Has the puppy been registered with the Kennel Club (if pedigree)?
13. How old is the puppy?
14. Is the puppy fully weaned?
15. Is the puppy healthy?
16. Has the puppy started his vaccinations? Can I see his vaccination card?
17. Has the puppy been wormed?
18. Is the puppy microchipped?
19. What is the puppy being fed?
20. What socialization has the puppy had?
21. May I see where the dogs are kept, where they sleep, and where the puppies were born?
22. May I have the details of your vet?
23. Can I return the puppy if it has any health problems, or things don't work out?
24. Can I visit several times before bringing my puppy home? (A good breeder will encourage this.)

CHAPTER 4   How to Choose a Labrador Retriever

Good breeders also have just as much of an interest in making sure their puppies go to good homes as you have in purchasing a top-quality puppy. So, don't be surprised if you are asked questions too!

Inquire about the Parents

"Be sure that the breeder has health certified the breeding pair through PennHip and the Orthopedic Foundation for Animals for hip and elbow dysplasia and heart valve determination at the age of two years. Breeder should also be doing genetic testing through agencies such as PawPrintGenetics or Optigen for heritable problems such as HNPK (peeling nose), PRA, PRA-rcd (eye disorders), EIC (exercise induced collapse), CNM (centronuclear myopathy) nervous system disorder which cause the back end to go out. Certificates are issued by the agencies to prove the genetic testing has been done and issued to the breeder."

Lori Lutz
Bowery Run Labradors

You should ask the breeder about the health tests he carries out on his breeding stock, as Labradors can be subject to so many inherited conditions. The minimum health tests for Labradors required by the USA Labrador Retriever Club and the Orthopedic Foundation for Animals Canine Health Information Center (OFA-CHIC) are:

- Hip scores
- Elbow scores
- An eye examination
- A DNA test for Exercise Induced Collapse
- A DNA for the dilute coat gene (mentioned in Chapter 2)
- Other optional tests include a heart examination and DNA tests for Centronuclear Myopathy and prcd-PRA.

You should ideally ask the breeder to email or post copies of these health tests before you go to look at the puppies.

Hip scores range from 0 to 106 (53 on each hip). It is expressed as two numbers, and the lower the score the better. Breeders should only be breeding from parents that score below the breed average, and for a Labrador, this is 12, or 6:6. As well as a low number, you should be looking for even numbers on both sides.

Elbow scores are rated 0-3. Zero is a perfect elbow, so both parents should ideally score 0.

Photo Courtesy of Megan Seliger

CHAPTER 4   How to Choose a Labrador Retriever

The breeder should also send you a copy of the parents' pedigrees, and you should look for as little inbreeding as possible. This is because genetic variation protects against inherited diseases.

Other things to check in advance concern the general welfare of the dogs. You should ask where the dogs live. This may be kennels or in the home. If in the home, the puppies will be well adapted to the home environment when you bring your puppy home. If in a kennel, more common with working dogs, the puppies should still be given some time each day inside the home. You should inspect the dogs' living environment when you visit.

A good breeder should have the utmost concern for the health of his breeding females. So, you should check that the mother has had no more than one litter in a 12-month period, and that she has had no more than three litters in her lifetime. She should be between the age of two to eight years at the time of whelping.

Ask the breeder about his aftercare and support. A good breeder will always remain contactable in the event of any problems or to offer advice. Some will even offer vacation boarding. Most reputable breeders will always take a puppy back if things don't work out, or you are no longer able to care for it. However, this is no excuse for taking a puppy on lightly, and the breeder will be looking for the measure of your commitment before releasing one of his precious pups into your care.

A word of caution: if you decide to bypass the Kennel Club Assured Breeders list and buy a Labrador puppy from a private seller, you should be acutely aware of the pitfalls.

Everyone has heard of the term "puppy farm" or "puppy mill" and is confident they would spot one from a mile off. However, many unlicensed breeders will show their puppies in a clean front room that is a world away from the squalid and overcrowded sheds round the back where their dogs are actually kept. And if you are shown any pedigrees or certificates at all, they may not actually belong with the parents. Buying a cheap Labrador puppy is likely to cost you dearly in the future when your dog succumbs to his poor genetic inheritance. And it perpetuates animal suffering, so there is nothing more important to animal welfare, and your own pocket in the long term, than supporting responsible breeding.

Looking at the Puppy

The three most important qualities you need to consider in your puppy should be inherited from the parents, and they are temperament, health and ability. You may or may not have the chance to meet the father of the puppies, but you will have seen his documents to satisfy yourself as to his health and ability. You should always see the mother, however, so you will be able to assess her temperament too. This is the best guide, as when you first meet your puppy at 5-8 weeks, it will not be easy to spot how he will turn out. You may however note that some puppies are assertive, and others may be quieter. The breed standard states that a Labrador Retriever should be outgoing and never shy. But if in doubt, it is a good rule of thumb to look for the dog that seems midway between the two extremes if you do not want to have to deal with either dominance or fearfulness.

You may already have an idea of whether you would prefer a male or female Labrador Retriever. Fortunately, with this easygoing breed, there is little difference in temperament whichever you choose, especially if you plan to neuter your dog. A female Labrador will come into season twice a year, which can be messy and inconvenient. So, unless you plan to breed from her yourself, which is not recommended unless you intend to join the Kennel Club Approved Breeders, then it is best to have your female dog spayed after her first season. This will also protect her from a deadly uterus infection called pyometra that can affect unspayed females.

It is also a good idea to neuter your male Labrador if you do not intend to breed from him, as it will make him less inclined to roam, and potentially gentler by nature. Plus, he will not become an unintended father!

If you have no experience of puppies, it is a good idea to take a knowledgeable friend with you to view the litter. This will help make sure your heart does not rule your head, and you are looking for all the hallmarks of a healthy puppy. Although if you are buying from a registered breeder you should expect all the puppies to be meeting this standard.

You should watch the breeder pick up the puppies, and they should be accepting of being handled. The breeder should then let you pick up the puppies to check their physical health. You should ensure that a puppy's eyes, ears and bottom are clean and free from discharge. His coat should be silky with no scabs, and his tummy should be plump but not hard. Check there is no lump on his tummy which may be an umbilical hernia, and if you are looking at a boy, check that he has two descended testicles, although these may not be evident until you collect him after 8 weeks, and sometimes even later than that.

CHAPTER 4   How to Choose a Labrador Retriever

When you pick up your puppy, he should come with a comprehensive puppy pack, containing your contract of sale, your dog's registration certificate and pedigree, immunization record, worming record, and advice for continuation of care, socialization, exercise and training. You will also receive a contractual guarantee, detailing any conditions that may apply if you need to return a puppy.

As soon as possible after collecting your puppy, you should take him to your vet for a full physical examination. This will ensure you have not missed anything that may affect the health of your dog, and it will get him registered with your vet for the continuation of his vaccinations and on-going health care. You should try to avoid forming too much of an attachment to your puppy until the vet has given him the all-clear, as he will be with you for potentially the next twelve years or more, so it has to be the right decision.

Photo Courtesy of Donna Launonen

Considerations of a Rescue Dog

If you have decided to adopt rather than buy your Labrador Retriever, you first need to identify a shelter that has Labradors. Most shelters have a website where you can view the dogs that are available for adoption, and they will come with a short assessment of their background, temperament, and the sort of home to which they would be suited. As well as mixed-breed shelters, you may find a shelter in your area that specializes in Labradors and Retrievers. The advantage of a specialized rescue organization is they are very experienced in the breed, and able to assess the dogs and their needs, so you will have a reliable indication of what you are taking on, and the rescue may be better able to make a perfect match.

When you have identified a dog, or a shortlist of dogs, that you are interested in, the rescue organization will ask you to complete an application form. This is likely to ask about your personal circumstances, experience, and some details of your home. Most reputable rescues will then assign a home checker to visit your home, irrespective of whether or not you are a novice or experienced dog owner. This is part of their duty of care to the dogs for which they have taken responsibility, and it is partly to check your identity and home address, and partly just to make sure your living space is adequate and safe for the dog. If the home checker notices anything that needs attention, for example a fence that is too low or has a gap, or hazardous materials in the yard, the rescue will ask you to fix these before you can take the dog.

Photo Courtesy of Tom Morgan

When you pick up your dog, you will be asked to pay an adoption fee. This may be almost as much as the price of purchasing a puppy, but it serves several important purposes. Firstly, the fee is a measure of your commitment to the dog, and also ensures no one goes to a rescue to pick up a free dog for fighting, breeding or selling on. Secondly,

CHAPTER 4   How to Choose a Labrador Retriever

Photo Courtesy of Amy Seto

your rescue dog has come at a financial price to the organization, as a reputable rescue will have paid for veterinary care, microchipping, vaccinations, parasite treatment, neutering, feed, kenneling and transport.

A good rescue organization will provide ongoing support for you and your dog throughout its life, and as part of the adoption agreement, if your circumstances should ever change, you will be obliged to return the dog to the rescue for rehoming rather than find it another home yourself. This is because a rescue commits to the welfare of the dog for life, to ensure it is never let down again, and the same careful checks will be made on the dog's next home as were made on yours.

A rescue dog may come with health issues due to poor breeding or previous neglect. It may also come with psychological scars and may not have been well trained from an early age. So, in taking on a rescue dog, you will probably have additional work to do to turn your four-legged friend's life around. Training classes can provide expertise and moral support, and your vet is also a valued source of advice. The rescue is also there to help you, and they may be able to put you in touch with a behaviorist if you need one. You should never feel too proud to ask for help, as everybody wants to make the partnership work.

Fortunately, Labradors are naturally friendly and trainable, and most people do not encounter persistent problems with the breed. So, you have the best chance of enjoying many happy and fulfilled years with your rescue Labrador. And he will never hold back in letting you know how much he appreciates it!

CHAPTER 5
Preparations for a New Dog

"Lab puppies are work and require a fair amount of time very early on, so be sure your schedule is clear for the first month you bring them home. Try to limit any vacations/travel and visitors so you can properly bond with your puppy. Eight to twelve weeks is a critical bonding period."

Neil and Jodi Martin
Carriage Hill Labradors

Preparing Your Home

"Crawl around on the floor and look for anything that can be chewed. Wires are a favorite for pups and can cause electrocution. Be sure to get lots of toys for redirection and make a safe zone for the pup to be in when you can't be watching them."

Jennifer Robinson
Chestnut's Labs2Love

Whether you are buying a puppy or adopting a Labrador from a shelter, there will be a few weeks leading up to the day you bring your dog home, and this is the time to make sure your home is ready to welcome your new arrival.

Even if you already have a dog and think your yard is secure, you need to think about the dog you will be bringing home, as he may have a totally new set of escape methods. Whether you are bringing home a puppy or an adult dog, your yard is not yet his territory and he doesn't know the boundaries. He also hasn't yet bonded with you as his master and provider, so he has no motive to stay by your side. So, any gaps in your fences need to be closed up, or your dog will head for the hills at the first opportunity, especially a Labrador. If you are bringing home a puppy, you need to be especially conscious of escape routes under your fences, and if you are adopting an adult Labrador, you need to ensure your fences are high enough that he doesn't jump out. Six feet is the recommended height.

Labradors have a natural instinct to roam, especially unneutered males, and until you have trained your dog to remain within his territory, you can't leave your dog unattended in the yard unless you have totally secured your boundary.

Remember too, that a Labrador is a pedigree dog and a target for dog thieves. You should make sure your back gate is locked at all times. If your gate does not have a lock, make sure you get one before you bring your dog home.

If you are a gardener or you have children that play in the yard, you will have to accept that from now on, your yard will also be your dog's bathroom and play space, and that he may dig holes and eat plants, regardless of whether or not they are toxic. So, if your yard is big enough, consider perhaps dividing it, so that you can still have your gardening area, and the chil-

dren can still play safely away from any poop that you may have missed. In your dog's area, you could create a sandpit for him to indulge his urge to dig in a space where he can't cause damage.

You will want to clear away your dog's mess on a daily basis, so you might think about where you will dispose of it, and have a poop scoop ready for the task.

If you use chemical methods of pest control, such as slug pellets, ant traps or rat bait, or chemical fertilizers, these should no longer be used in the parts of your yard which your dog has access to. You may consider more natural methods of pest control and organic gardening. Also, if you grow fruits and vegetables, make sure your Labrador does not have access to onions, grape vines, stone fruits, broccoli, rhubarb, unripe tomatoes, or the green tops of potato plants.

If you have any hazards in your yard, such as panes of glass, garbage, or fungi, these should be removed before your dog arrives. If you are adopting, these will probably have been highlighted during the home check. But if you are buying your first puppy, you could ask an experienced dog-owning friend to check your yard to see if you have missed anything.

Inside the home, you should think about whether you want your new dog to have the run of the house, or to restrict him to certain areas. It is always best to start with restrictions and relax them later on, rather than impose restrictions once your dog has got used to total freedom. Also,

CHAPTER 5 Preparations for a New Dog

when you are housetraining your dog, it is useful if he can be kept mostly to rooms with hard floors that are easy to clean. If you plan to crate train your dog, then you should think about where to place the crate. This will be your dog's sleeping area at night, so it should be away from drafts. But your dog will also like to have company when he uses his crate during the day, so the kitchen or a corner of the living room usually works best. Your dog should see his crate as his safe space, so leaving the door open and letting him choose to go in, is the way to acceptance. You can make your dog's crate attractive to him by putting in a soft blanket, toys and safe chews.

Inspect the rooms where your dog is going to be allowed, and think about whether you need to remove anything that your dog will destroy or that may be hazardous to him. These include breakables, gadgets with batteries, shoes, children's toys, books, medicines, food, and anything you particularly value. Remember, teething makes your Labrador want to chew, but boredom will make him even more destructive. He could even destroy the couch or the door frames if he suffers separation anxiety. Crate training your Lab from the start is a good idea, and having a safe space can make him less anxious and more inclined to settle.

If you are taking on a puppy, there will definitely be messes in the house in the early days, and even if you are adopting an adult Labrador, you may need to do some potty training, especially if he has only ever lived in a kennel. If you have hard floors, cleaning will be quick and easy, but if you have carpets, it's worth investing in a carpet shampooer and an enzymatic cleaner to deal promptly with any accidents. You could even consider taking the carpets up for the first few months. Labradors are quick to learn though, so you should soon have potty training mastered. Some tips for this are given in Chapter 6.

Collecting your dog is likely to involve his first ever car journey, and he may experience motion sickness on the way home. He is also likely to pee or poop. So be sure to put a few old towels in the car and some wipes, as well as a bowl and bottle of water if the journey is a long one. Chapter 7 covers traveling with your dog, and will help you decide where in the car you wish him to travel. Your dog should always be restrained in the car, for his own safety, and so that he doesn't cause an accident. This is a legal requirement in some countries. So, you will need to think ahead and purchase a crate or harness for your dog's first trip home.

A bit of foresight during the exciting weeks leading up to your new dog's homecoming will deal with any problems before they occur, and ensure he fits into your family and home right away!

Shopping List

"Mental stimulation is just as great as physical exercise, so get puzzle toys, treat dispensing balls, hide toys for your dog to find, etc."

Tiffany Ginkel
Cedar Ranch Labrador Retrievers

If this is your first dog, the list of things to get for him may seem overwhelming. But whereas certain things are basic essentials, most of the accessories you will see in the pet store are luxuries that you may like to purchase later, but you don't need from the start. Here we will run through your basic requirements.

Crates

To begin with, whether or not you plan to crate train your puppy, a crate is still useful for all sorts of reasons. To start with, it may be your preferred method of traveling your dog in the car. It is also useful to have in the home as your dog's safe space, even if you never shut him in. It can separate your dog if he needs time out from the children or other dogs. And if he gets injured or sick, he may need crate rest for a short time while he gets better.

You can buy metal or fabric crates, but whether you are getting a puppy or a rescue dog, a metal crate is best because it withstands chewing. You can get special covers for metal crates to help your dog settle at night, or you can just use a towel or blanket. If you are going to use your crate to potty train your Labrador, it is important not to buy one that is too large, even if he will grow into it. This is because a dog has an instinct not to soil his bed, but if his crate is large, he can just potty in the opposite corner, rather than wait to be let out in the yard. Dogs also prefer to feel fairly snug in their crate.

> **HELPFUL TIP**
> **Why Crate Training is a Good Thing**
>
> Some people think crate training is a terrible, cruel thing. In fact, it's a good idea to crate train your dog, even if you don't intend to keep them crated on a regular basis. You never know when you might need to crate or kennel your dog—for instance when you're traveling or if it gets injured—and you don't want it to be panicked about being in a crate in addition to whatever situation put them there.

CHAPTER 5 Preparations for a New Dog

Photo Courtesy of Christianna Legner

This means you may have to start with a medium crate, and buy a large one when your dog grows. But you can always buy secondhand, and sell your old crate when you move up a size.

Beds

Your Labrador will also need a bed. Even if he is going to sleep in his crate at night, he may still appreciate a bed in another part of the house to use during the day when he wants to be by your side. As with the crate, your Labrador puppy will outgrow his bed in time, so there is no point investing in anything too expensive, especially as he is likely to chew it. For this reason, plastic beds are ideal for puppies. You can make them comfy with old towels or blankets. Padded fabric beds may look cozier, but your dog is sure to pull the stuffing out for his own entertainment, so he can graduate to a more luxurious bed later. Not only can the stuffing make a mess, Labradors are prone to eating everything, and therefore stuffing can pose a real risk for gastrointestinal blockages.

Photo Courtesy of
Brittany Pescara
Black Swamp Labradors

CHAPTER 5 Preparations for a New Dog

Collars, Harnesses and Leashes

The next things you will need are a collar, harness and leash. Collars and harnesses are usually adjustable, so as long as you can make them small enough for your dog, they will still fit him for a good while as he grows. It is recommended that your dog wears a collar, as it carries his ID tag, which you should also have on hand before he arrives in your home. This is because the early days are when your Lab is most likely to stray or run off. Your dog's ID tag should have your current cell phone number as a minimum. Your address is optional, but ID tags do not generally carry the dog's name. If your dog isn't microchipped, you should ask your vet to insert a chip at your first appointment, as this is a form of identification that cannot fall off or be removed by thieves, and could lead to the return of your dog after theft or straying. Microchipping is further discussed in Chapter 11.

A harness is also recommended for two reasons. Firstly, a dog may easily slip his collar, but is less likely to wriggle out of a harness, and secondly, a harness spreads the pull of the lead across the chest, rather than tugging at the delicate neck area. Although your Labrador will learn to walk on a loose leash, he is sure to pull on it to start with, and you need to guard against him hurting his neck. For the same reason, you should never purchase a choke chain, or attend a training class where this harsh method is used.

The only leash you will require at this stage is a short, clip-on leash made from fabric webbing or leather. There is no need to purchase a flexi-leash, as you will be training your Labrador to walk nicely on a short leash, and will be teaching him reliable recall so he can enjoy himself off leash. Flexi-leashes do have their uses but can also cause accidents. You may consider purchasing a long line for recall training but this is optional, and discussed in Chapter 6.

Bowls

The only other essentials your dog will need at this stage are food and water bowls. These do not need to be from the pet store, but they should be heavy to avoid being pushed around the floor. Your new dog may come to you with some of his regular food, especially if you are buying a puppy. If not, you should ask what the dog is currently being fed, and continue with his regular diet while he settles in. If you choose to switch him to a different diet in the weeks to come, this should be done gradually. There is more about nutrition in Chapter 8.

Photo Courtesy of Kristin Daniello

CHAPTER 5   Preparations for a New Dog

Introducing Your New Labrador Retriever to Other Dogs

"When introducing a new puppy to other pets always do it in a neutral zone of the home away from food bowls, prized toys, or favorite sleeping areas. Straddle the puppy on your forearm with rear end facing outward for other animal to sniff. Be sure to have the other animal(s) on leash and held by another person in case a pull-away is necessary. If more than one dog is in the home, introduce only one at a time. Put puppy in crate for protection and allow other animals to circle the crate off leash to sniff through the crate. Do not put the puppy on the floor unless you are completely confident that the other animals will not attack out of jealousy or fear."

Lori Lutz
Bowery Run Labradors

If you already have a dog, you may be looking forward to bringing home a new friend for him, and in most cases the dogs will get along fine; however, it may not be love at first sight. This is because your resident dog sees your house as his territory, and your family as exclusively his humans. He may not be so willing to share with the newcomer. Also, if your resident dog is elderly, and you are bringing a puppy home, older dogs can be quite intolerant to puppies, and puppies may be disrespectful towards other dogs while they are still learning the rules. So careful introductions are important, to make sure the new relationship gets off to the best start.

If you are adopting a rescue dog from a shelter, he may have already met your resident dog at a "meet-and-greet." Rescues often like to get a measure of how their dog will get on with yours, but to keep it as stress-free as possible, a meet-and-greet will usually take place at a neutral location, away from the territory of your own home. So even if your dogs have gotten along just fine at the meet-and-greet, they now need to learn to share their living space and their humans for the first time.

The worst place for your new dog to come face to face with your resident dog for the first time is on the doorstep. This is an immediate confrontation and puts your resident dog on the defensive, because an unknown dog is about to enter his territory. When you bring your new dog home, you should take him to the back yard. If your yard can only be accessed through the house, get a friend or family member to take your resident dog out for a walk when you are due to arrive. Allow your new dog to get acquainted with the yard, just long enough for him to process his new surroundings, then let your resident dog out calmly and without fuss. Be prepared for a range of reactions to follow in rapid succession, possibly from shock to curiosity to excitement to rebuke to chasing and hopefully to playing and acceptance. You should stand back and let the dogs sort it out, but be prepared only to intervene if you notice the warning signs of aggression. In most cases, a first encounter in the yard will be fairly uneventful, as the resident dog doesn't know that the newcomer is here to stay, he may just be on a play date. So, he is not feeling as defensive as if the first encounter had happened in the house.

If you have no secure yard, or the weather is bad, or there is some other reason why the introduction cannot take place outside, then there is still a correct way to manage first introductions in the house or apartment. In this case, the resident dog should be taken out for a walk while the new dog is brought into the home, and given enough time to process his environment and settle down. Then your resident dog should be brought calmly back into the house to find the newcomer already there and settled. Again, the initial encounter may be tense, and there may even be some scrapping, but you should stay calm and avoid overreacting while the dogs get acquainted with each other. If you have children, it is a good idea for them to be elsewhere while your dogs meet each other for the first time, as you do not want to add any more excitement into the encounter than necessary.

Once your puppy's vaccinations are complete, he can go out to the park and meet other dogs of all ages. However, it is vitally important that your puppy doesn't have a negative experience of socialization, and as puppies can be rather over-the-top, they may try the patience of some dogs, especially seniors. So always keep the encounters short and positive, with the full permission of the other dog owners. Early socialization should be on-leash, so you can extract your puppy easily if things look ready to turn bad.

You should always be aware of canine body language in supervising encounters with other dogs. It is natural for two dogs to approach each other nose-to-nose, then turn to sniff the other end. They should appear relaxed, with a gently wagging tail. If the body and tail stiffen, or the tail starts to vibrate, the dog may be ready to snap, especially if the lips become drawn back. This is an immediate signal for you to end the encounter before a positive experience becomes a negative one and damages your puppy's confidence, or even causes injury.

CHAPTER 5 Preparations for a New Dog

Introducing Your New Labrador Retriever to Children

The Labrador Retriever is a great family dog, and in most instances will get along fine with children. However, the relationship between your dog and the kids starts first with teaching your children how to act around dogs.

If this is your first dog, and your children are quite young without much experience of being around dogs, you should use the time leading up to bringing your dog home in taking your children to visit friends with child-friendly dogs. These introductions should be very carefully steered by you, in order that the dogs are not placed under any stress. If your children cannot respect the rules of these introductions, then you may have to reconsider bringing a dog into your home at this stage.

Explain to your children that they should be very gentle when greeting a dog, and never run up to him or grab his ears or tail. Tell them to approach the dog from the side, talking to him gently to take care not to take him by surprise. Tell them to offer the dog a closed fist to sniff, and then show your children the places on a dog's body where he will enjoy being stroked, on the back of his neck and back. Make sure that your children know they should not try to pet the dog while he is eating or sleeping. If your children are older, you can explain about a dog's body language and how to spot the warning signs of aggression, as explained in the previous section. Also, you should aim to involve your children in your dog's care, walking, feeding and grooming your dog, so that your new dog learns to respect your children as part of the team that provides for his needs.

If your Labrador Retriever is dominant by nature, then there is always a risk he will try to infiltrate the hierarchy of the household by assuming second place below you and your partner, but ahead of the children. This can lead to him growling or snarling at the children, or even snapping, despite it not being part of the natural behavior of a Labrador. Involving your children in the dog's care, and especially his training, will help to address this issue. If your dog is inclined to be dominant, make sure that he sleeps downstairs and never in the bedrooms, especially not on the master bed, as this will just tell him he is the boss and can make up the house rules.

Luckily, the Labrador is not an aggressive dog by nature, and in many ways, he completes the family. For a child, growing up with a dog teaches respect, kindness, gentleness and responsibility. It also encourages physical exercise. And having a Labrador in the family can define a kid's childhood, and create a memory that will always bring joy to look back on.

CHAPTER 6
Training

"Start training as soon as you bring your puppy home, nothing will hurt their progress like letting them get away with bad behavior until they are six months old."

Kathy Jackson
Karemy Labs

CHAPTER 6 Training

Whether you are bringing home a puppy or a rescue Labrador Retriever, you will need to do some training with your new arrival. A Labrador Retriever is naturally smart and trainable, so in many respects, progress with a puppy may be quicker than retraining an older dog that has ingrained behaviors. If you have trained dogs before, you will have your own tried and tested methods, but if you are new to dog training or would just appreciate some support, it's a great idea to join a training class. You should stick with whatever methods your training class uses, so as not to confuse your dog. But if you are training your dog at home, there are some excellent online tutorials demonstrating how to teach all the basic commands.

ENCOURAGEMENT
How Many Commands Can You Teach Your Dog?

Dogs are capable of learning and understanding hundreds of words and commands. Make it a game to see how many different words and commands you can teach your Lab. They are one of the smartest dog breeds, after all, and make excellent service dogs.

Although there are many different training methods out there, the important thing to note is that harsh training methods, for example those that use choke chains or punishment, have been discredited and are known not to work. This is because they will create a fearful dog and may even cause physical injury, not to mention damage your relationship. These days, the training methods that are most highly recommended use positive reinforcement. This means that your dog is rewarded for the correct action, thereby learning what you require of him. Positive reinforcement makes your dog eager to learn and strengthens your bond. The reward that you give to your dog may simply be praise, or his favorite toy, but usually involves a small food treat reward. For a dog like a Labrador, this is a huge incentive, which may be one reason the Labrador is one of the most trainable dog breeds in the world! Do remember to adjust your dog's regular food portion size while you are using food rewards, as Labradors are prone to weight gain.

Training treats are commercially available, but you can use small pieces of sausage or dried liver chips. However, for a Labrador, even his normal kibble will be motivation enough!

Clicker training is also a popular training method. This is just the same as positive reinforcement, or reward-based training, but as well as the reward, the owner uses a clicker for each correct action. This is an additional signal to the dog that he has done the right action, and food treats may gradually be reduced in favor of the clicker alone.

A brief summary of how to train your dog is given in this chapter.

Potty Training

"Use the crate training method. If you're not home or can't watch the puppy, put it in a crate. It might sound mean, but Labs end up loving their crate and look at it as a place of security. Also never let them have an accident inside the house or they will go to that same spot, smell it and go potty again. When you get puppy out if it's crate, or when it's done eating, take it straight outside to the same area every time."

Lauren McNeely
Bayard Acres Labrador Retrievers

If you have brought home a Labrador puppy, potty training will be the first thing he needs to learn. If you have rescued your Labrador, he may already be clean in the house, but many rescue dogs are not, either because they have never been properly trained, or they have always lived outdoors. Training an older dog can be harder work, but you have two things in your favor: it is natural for a dog to keep his sleeping area clean, and you are training a Labrador, who by nature is quick to learn.

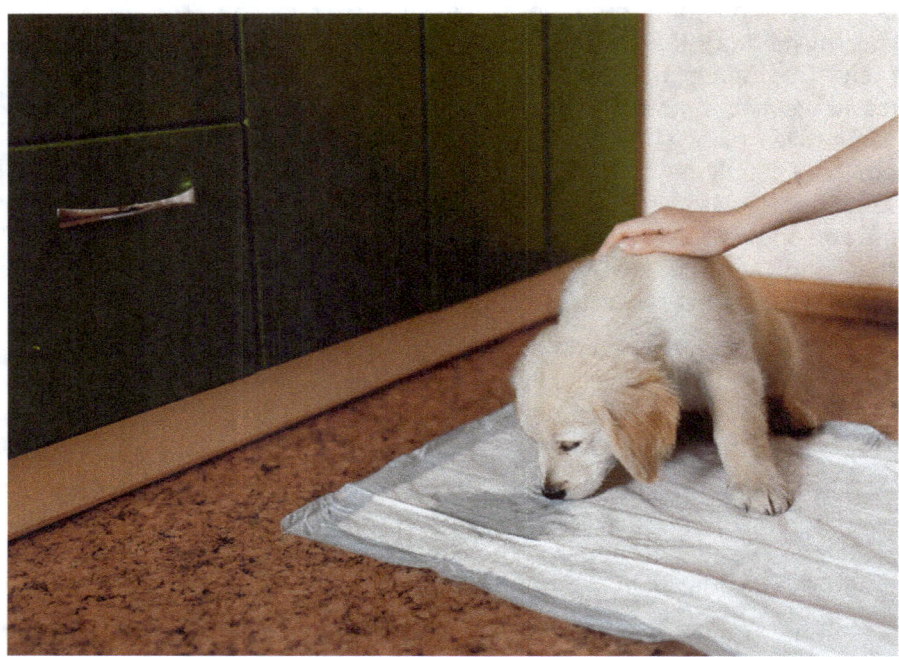

CHAPTER 6   Training

It is because of a dog's instinct to keep his sleeping area clean that many people favor crate training. If your dog accepts a crate, which most puppies will, although some older dogs may not, then he will instinctively avoid messing in it, as long as he is given plenty of opportunities to relieve himself outdoors.

There are two things to note with crate training; first, if your crate is too big, your dog can simply potty in the opposite corner to his bed, and second, it is vital not to keep him hanging on if he needs to potty, especially with a puppy who has not yet developed muscle control. So do take your dog out into the yard every hour to begin with. This is where you will train him to potty on command.

Teaching command words to your dog is known as associative training, and you are basically teaching him human language. So, to achieve this, in the training stage, you need to use the command word only when he is performing the correct action, and not before it. This is so he associates the word with the action by constant repetition and reward. Once the word is cemented in his brain as associated with the action, you will be able to use it as a command, to ask him for the correct action. This process can't be rushed, as if you use the word as a command before the dog has made the association, he will begin to associate it with running around doing his own thing, and your work will be undone.

Teaching a dog to potty appropriately takes patience. For some dogs, it comes naturally and only takes a matter of days, whereas others may take several weeks to understand that they should potty outside. To begin with, you are working with your dog's natural instincts not to soil his bed, and to potty when he feels the grass under his paws. Also, most dogs, particularly males, will instinctively cover another animal scent with their own urine, so that is another incentive to potty outside.

In the early days of potty training, you will simply take your dog outside for his potty break, and wait patiently, observing your dog closely for the first sign he is about to potty. With a puppy this may just be squatting as male puppies do not necessarily cock a leg at this stage. When you are confident your dog is beginning to potty, you can use your chosen command word. This can be anything you feel comfortable with, as long as you are consistent and it doesn't sound similar to your other command words. "Busy" is a popular command word for toileting. When your dog has finished, you should give him lots of fuss and a small treat to show him he has done the right thing.

If you are not crate training, you will need to watch your dog closely in the house, as if he gets used to toileting indoors you will lose the initiative. Take him out frequently, and if you see him preparing to potty indoors, whisk him outside quickly. If you are too late, you should never scold your dog, as it will make him fearful and he may potty more through stress. Just clean the area thoroughly with an enzymatic cleaner to break down the ammonia, as dogs are drawn back to areas where they smell this natural chemical, and it can lead to repeat marking.

The use of puppy pads or newspaper indoors is not recommended, as they give the dog permission to potty indoors, and the dog learns that a soft texture under his paws is OK to relieve himself. This can lead to toileting on carpets and furniture. Your dog needs to learn that only grass or earth under his paws gives him permission to potty.

Your Labrador is sure to learn quickly because he is smart. However, if at a later stage you notice him regress and start pottying indoors again, you should take him to your vet for a check over. He may have an illness or infection. Or sometimes, he may be under psychological stress, which could be helped by your vet or a behaviourist. It is very rarely your Labrador's fault, as all he really wants is to please you.

CHAPTER 6 Training

How to Teach Sit

"Always keep training sessions for sit, down, fetch to no longer than ten minutes for puppies and helpful to do training just before mealtime so they appreciate the reward."

Lori Lutz
Bowery Run Labradors

"Sit" is an important command to teach your Labrador, because it creates a situation where the dog is focused and static, ready for any additional commands that may follow. It is also an important command for your dog's own safety. "Sit" is an easy command for your dog to learn, and in being rewarded for his achievement, he will be eager for the next steps in his education!

To begin teaching your dog anything, you need his full attention. Puppies are full of energy, so this may be a challenge at first; however, your Labrador is likely to be very focused if you have a tasty treat in your hand, ready for him to earn. If you are training a puppy, you should be kneeling on the floor at his level.

Begin by teaching, "Look at Me" to your dog. To earn the treat, all your dog has to do to earn his reward is make sustained eye contact with you. After several repetitions, he should be getting the idea that it's time for class.

With your dog's attention focused on you, bring your hand with the treat enclosed towards your dog's nose. Now, with a smooth motion, bring the treat over the back of your dog's head. With this, your dog's hind quarters will instinctively lower. When his bottom hits the floor, this is when you use the command word "Sit" and give him the treat and some fuss.

If your dog does not instinctively sit with this action, but spins or jumps about, you should remain patient. You shouldn't force your dog into the sitting position, but can gently guide his hindquarters with your free hand. When he has done it right a few times, he will get the idea, and several more repetitions will fix it in his mind.

As your training progresses, you can wean your dog off the hand signal, by making it smaller. At this stage, your dog has made the connection with the word "Sit." So, you will get to the stage that you can use the command word before the action, to ask for a sit. You can then treat him. But

Photo Courtesy of Fernando Yoc

in due course, you can wean him off the treat as well, so that praise alone is his reward.

You don't have to reach all these stages in one training session. In fact, for most dogs, reaching all the stages in one training session is impossible. On average, it will take several weeks to learn the basics, and a further few months to reinforce them. Keep the sessions short for your dog and end on a positive note. Build training into his daily routine so it soon becomes second nature, and it will not be a chore for either of you.

How to Teach Stay

Stay is a potentially life-saving command to teach your dog. It requires great obedience from him as you are asking him to override his instinct, which may be to follow you, run around, or to chase whatever it is that has caught his eye.

Along with the Stay command, you also need to teach a command to release your dog from the Stay. A good word for this is "Free." You need to control both the stay and the release, so that your dog takes his instructions from you, and doesn't start thinking he can end the stay when he pleases.

Step 1: To teach Stay, first put your dog in the Sit position, which means he is still, focused, and ready to learn.

Step 2: You can then use the word "Stay," as he is staying, but don't reward him yet or he will think his job is done.

Step 3: You will then release him by leading him away from the Sit with a treat in your hand.

Step 4: Immediately he gets up, use the word "Free."

Once you have taught your dog to associate the word with the action, you can release your dog with just the word "Free" and no hand action, and then give him the treat and some fuss.

When your dog has mastered the concept of Stay and Free, you should put him in the Stay, then walk a few paces before releasing him. If he tries to follow you, return and put him back in the Stay. If this doesn't come naturally to your dog, you can ask a helper to hold your dog's collar as you move away, and let go as you release him. As he learns the pattern, your helper can let go earlier, then step back, and finally no longer be required. Increase the distance you move away, and the time you hold your dog in the Stay, as your training progresses, eventually moving out of sight of your dog while he remains in the Stay.

How to Teach Lie Down

To teach your Labrador Retriever to lie down, you first need to ask him to Sit. Kneel in front of your dog, and be sure you have his full attention. Show him that you have a treat in your closed hand by bringing it to his nose, then immediately down towards the floor between his legs. Your dog should then instinctively drop his front legs, and once his elbows hit the floor, you can reward him, but don't use the command word yet.

The next stage is to get his hind quarters to lower as well, so that he is lying down. He may already have lowered both his front legs and hind quarters at stage one, but if not, once his front legs are down, use your free hand like a limbo pole over his back, and draw the treat towards you, so that he has to creep forward. This will cause his hind quarters to lower under the limbo pole, and you should achieve a lying down position. If it doesn't happen straight away, just be patient, and keep repeating the exercise. You can reward each step of progress your dog makes, but don't use the command "Lie Down" until you actually achieve the correct position. Then repeat several more times to fix the command in your Labrador's brain.

How to Teach Walk On the Leash

Teaching your Labrador Retriever to walk nicely on a loose leash is very important, as he is going to grow into a powerful dog, and you do not want to be that owner who is being dragged around the park by their headstrong dog. Pulling on the leash is bad for your dog and can cause injury, and it can also cause injury to you. It also undermines your relationship with your dog, who should be respecting your rules. So even though your Labrador puppy thinks the leash is something to be bitten and played with, the sooner you start leash training with him, the better.

If you have adopted a dog that has never been trained to walk properly on a leash, you will have ingrained behavior to overcome, but the same basic premise applies, whatever the age of your Labrador. Your dog is going to learn that if he wants to go forward, this will only happen with a loose leash. When he pulls, you stop. This can seem very tedious to start off with, and you may never get very far, but it really is worth persevering.

To encourage your dog to focus on you rather than pulling on the leash, you should aim to be exciting and full of encouragement. Of course, if you have treats in your pocket, most Labradors will find that very exciting, so you can keep slipping your dog a food reward all the while he is walking

CHAPTER 6 Training

nicely. For this exercise, you should be using a short leash attached to a collar, with your dog on your left, and the leash in your right hand. This leaves your left hand free on the dog's side to keep the treats coming.

Don't let your dog assume which direction you are going. He needs to be looking to you for the cues. Keep changing direction, and keep being interesting. And just as before, keep your training sessions short, so you can end on a positive note before your dog's concentration flags.

If your dog has been learning walking on the leash in a training class environment, and he appears to be doing well, don't be disheartened if you find he becomes difficult as soon as you try to walk him outdoors. There are obviously many more distractions outside, so this is the next step in his training. Just be patient and keep up the exercises on a daily basis, and your Labrador will learn that walking on the leash means walking nicely by your side.

How to Teach Walk Off the Leash

The Labrador Retriever was bred as a working dog, so it is natural for him to want to run freely in the countryside, exploring his surroundings, burning off his boundless energy and exercising his busy mind. This he would happily do all day, however, your Labrador can run for miles, so you need to be able to recall him instantly for his own safety. Good recall is vitally important for a Labrador so that he can enjoy all the freedom that comes with being a trustworthy dog.

All the early training you have done with your dog before he even saw the great outdoors, will set a firm foundation for your recall training, because it has established your relationship, and taught him that you are his master, provider and friend. So, it is in his interests to obey you, and being a Labrador, he really does want to please.

When you were teaching Stay and Free, you were preparing your dog for being off-leash, by giving him permission to move away on your terms. This exercise is a good way to start in a safely enclosed area, by sending your dog away for longer periods to run and explore, then calling him back with the "Come" command.

As with the previous commands, in order to make the association, you should not use the word until your dog is actually doing the action. So, in your safe space, send your dog away, then at the point he makes eye contact with you again, grab his full attention by holding out a treat and as he

comes towards you, call "Come" with much enthusiasm, and a lot of praise when he is back by your side.

If you do not have a fully enclosed safe space, or your dog is slower to respond, you can use a lightweight training line. These are very long lines that clip to a dog's harness and allow you to control the range your dog is allowed, and gently encourage his return alongside the treat and praise reward. You should only ever use a training leash off a harness, not a collar, in case he runs at speed to the end of it, which could cause a neck injury.

Initially you should call your dog back very frequently, and don't let him get too carried away with his own agenda. Also, change direction frequently, so that your dog has to stay focused on your position. If your dog does run off, try to avoid chasing after him, unless he is running into danger, as that is a game to him. Instead, you should turn in the opposite direction. When your dog notices you are moving away from him, this usually rattles him enough to come bounding back to your side.

Because the Labrador is a working dog, some people like to teach recall to a whistle. This can be an ordinary audible whistle, or a dog whistle, which is a high frequency whistle only audible to the dog. The whistle has the advantage of being audible over a long distance if your dog has run far. As working dogs usually have a considerable range, the whistle is a useful accessory, but you do need to remember always to carry it.

CHAPTER 6   Training

Agility and Flyball

Your Labrador Retriever is so athletic and intelligent that he could really enjoy the opportunity to exercise his body and mind in fun activities such as agility and flyball. These sports are high intensity and should never be attempted by puppies, due to the impact on their soft bones and undeveloped growth plates. But after your Labrador is one year old, he can begin low-impact agility training, progressing to the higher jumps after 18 months of age.

During the first year of your dog's life, all the obedience training you are doing with your dog is setting him up perfectly for agility and flyball, as he learns to focus on you, act on your commands, and gain the satisfaction of earning your praise. Agility is usually taught with a pocketful of training treats, so your Labrador will be highly motivated and quick to learn.

Flyball involves sending your dog round a circuit at high speed to retrieve a ball and then returning. Labradors love to run and retrieve, so your dog is likely to love flyball. Your earlier recall training will stand him in good stead for flyball, as unlike agility, he is running the course alone. This may suit you better if your own fitness prevents you running alongside your dog round an agility course.

Most Labradors will find agility and flyball hugely enjoyable, as the sports appeal to all their natural instincts and abilities. However, some more sensitive dogs may not enjoy the experience, and there is no value in causing stress to your dog. Also, if your dog has any orthopedic conditions such as hip or elbow dysplasia, or if he suffers from arthritis, he should not participate in impact sports or strenuous exercise. If you have any doubts, you should always ask your vet before signing up to agility or flyball training.

CHAPTER 7
Traveling

"Labs make great travel companions. They are easy going and get along with most people and pets. Most Labs love riding in cars."

Jennifer Robinson
Chestnut's Labs2Love

While the thought of taking your Labrador on vacation, or somewhere fun like a walk in the woods, might be an exciting prospect for you, your Labrador may not always agree. Some dogs travel excellently, while other dogs find the situation stressful or unpleasant for a variety of different reasons. Therefore, being prepared to travel will help the trip go smoothly and make it as enjoyable for your dog as possible. This chapter will look at all the different aspects of traveling with your dog, whether it's near or far, by plane or by car, and give you tips to help you be prepared for your trip.

CHAPTER 7   Traveling

Preparations for Travel

Preparing for traveling doesn't just start a few hours or days before the trip, but should begin when your dog is a puppy. Training your Labrador puppy to travel with confidence is vital for a stress-free trip. At the puppy stage, the main reason why dogs travel in the car is to go to the vet for their puppy vaccines, which associates traveling with a negative experience. Therefore, it is important to put in some effort right at the beginning to help your puppy associate the car with positive, fun times.

Start by introducing your puppy to the car. This can be as simple as opening the doors and letting him explore in his own time. When you have decided where your Labrador is likely to travel in the car, place him in that area and give him a treat. You can even make a habit of giving him a meal in that area, as one of a Labrador's favorite things to do is to eat! This will allow him to begin associating the car with something positive. After a few times of doing this, you can start introducing turning on the car ignition, shutting him in the car with you and then driving a very short distance, before working up to a longer journey.

Now that you have prepared your Labrador mentally for the journey, you should make practical preparations too. If you are going on a long trip that requires crossing borders, ensure that you know the regulations of the state or country you are traveling to. Your dog is likely to need a pet passport, which can be provided by your veterinarian. As a requirement for a

Photo Courtesy of John & Linda Ledwith

pet passport, your Labrador will need to be microchipped, if he isn't already, and be up to date with his vaccinations.

This is a good opportunity to visit your vet and ensure all is in order to travel. Some countries will require a rabies vaccination, followed by serology antibody titer testing, to ensure your dog has developed an immunity to rabies. Other countries will require a tapeworm treatment within 72 hours of travel. And if you are flying, instead of driving, the airline is likely to require a certificate of health provided by your veterinarian. Therefore, a check-up at your vet will help you make sure everything is in order, and allow you to pick up some flea or worming treatment if it is likely to lapse while you are away, or chronic medications if needed.

Once you are sure that your Labrador is ready to travel, it is important to make sure you are ready too. It is worth taking some time to look up the local veterinary practices in the area where you are staying, and key in the numbers into the contact list on your cell phone in case your dog needs emergency treatment while you are away. Also, contact the company where your dog's microchip is registered, to ensure that your details are up to date. That way if he becomes lost, he can always be traced back to you. An old cell number renders the microchip useless. If it puts your mind at ease, it can also be a good idea to put a temporary tag on your dog's collar with the address of where you are staying, although this is not as necessary as a tag with home details and the correct cell number.

CHAPTER 7 Traveling

Traveling in a Car

If your Labrador finds car rides stressful, and drools excessively, you should consider whether he might be experiencing motion sickness. This can be prevented by either traveling him on an empty stomach (if the journey is not too far), or asking your vet for travel sickness pills to give prior to the journey.

Photo Courtesy of Danielle Belmonte

Before setting off on your travels, you must decide how your dog is going to ride in the car. A popular and safe way for him to travel is with a dog car-seat harness. This is a harness which locks into the seatbelt clip when your dog is sitting on the back seat. As a result, your dog will be protected if you are in a collision. However, some people find that allowing their dog to ride in the back seat to be problematic. Not only does it get hair on the seats, but it also takes up the space where a person could be sitting. If cleanliness is the problem, then you can purchase a waterproof dog cover for the seat, which is particularly useful if you have taken your dog for a muddy walk or he's been for a swim (especially since Labradors have a strong affinity to muddy water!). If you prefer your dog to ride elsewhere in the car, most hatches have fitments where you can attach a harness.

There are also other options for where your Labrador can travel in the car. The hatch is an obvious choice for many. However, it is important that if you use this area for your dog, you should have a dog guard between the back seats and the hatch to prevent your Labrador from joining you in the front. This option also does not provide much protection for your dog if you are in an accident, as the hatch is prone to crumple in a rear-end collision. If you have a larger car, you might consider a crate in the hatch. This should be big enough for your Labrador to stand up in, turn around, and lie down comfortably without touching the sides. You can put a bed, towels or blankets in it to make it comfortable, and once used to it, your dog will probably find it to be a positive, comforting area to be.

When you travel long journeys in a car, ensuring your dog is comfortable is very important. This doesn't just mean that he has something comfortable to sit on, but that he has plenty of stops to run around, potty and have a drink of water. As a guideline, this should be at least every four hours. Food on a journey is less important, however if your journey is particularly long, you should allow him a small meal every 12 hours. Another comfort related factor to attend to is the temperature, especially if your car is not air-conditioned. Therefore, it is a good idea to travel in the coolest part of the day. You should never leave your dog in the car with no air conditioning and the windows up, as the temperatures can rise to dangerous levels in a matter of minutes. If you have to stop and leave him in the car, try to keep time to a minimum, ensure your car is parked in the shade and there is plenty of airflow to where your dog is sitting.

CHAPTER 7   Traveling

Photo Courtesy of Alex Adams

Photo Courtesy of Jordan Hohl

Traveling by Plane

Traveling by plane should not be undertaken lightly, however sometimes it is unavoidable. For example, you might be moving to another country or state and the distance is too far to drive. When traveling with your Labrador by air, there is a lot to think about, and you may find it helpful to enlist the services of a specialist pet carrier service who will deal with all the arrangements for you. These service providers are highly experienced, and will be able to provide you with a wealth of information to take away the stress.

When traveling by plane, small dogs and service dogs are allowed to travel in the cabin. However, most non-working Labradors will have to travel as cargo due to their size. Not all airlines are the same, and therefore researching the requirements specific to your flight will ensure the process goes as smoothly as possible. If your Labrador is younger than 12 weeks, or the forecast temperatures upon departure, arrival and during connections is particularly warm or cold, your dog may be refused travel.

If your Labrador has to travel as cargo, he will need to travel in an airline approved crate. Each airline will have different requirements for the size and structure of the crate, and it is your responsibility to make sure your dog's crate is suitable. Most airlines will also require a certificate of health or fitness to travel from your veterinarian, as well as a pet passport, and some destinations will require specific vaccines or export paperwork too. This is why it is important to do thorough research before traveling to ensure you have everything in place which is needed for travel.

Vacation Lodging

Before you book your accommodations, check that your Labrador is allowed to stay there too. Not all vacation lodging is pet friendly. It is also worth bearing in mind that even if your accommodations are pet friendly, not all guests will have pets, or even like animals, and therefore you should try to be courteous to everyone who is staying on site with you.

When you arrive, find out the rules. Some places will allow you to walk your dog around the premises freely, while others will prefer you to stay within your own area. They may also have preferences where you can take your dog to potty. Always make sure you clean up after your dog.

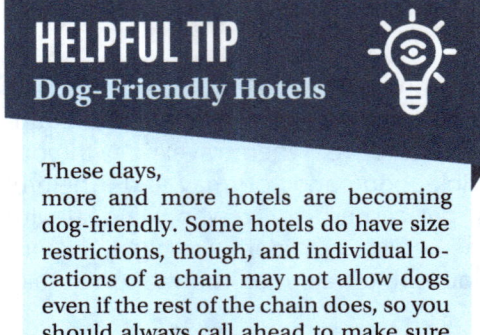

HELPFUL TIP
Dog-Friendly Hotels

These days, more and more hotels are becoming dog-friendly. Some hotels do have size restrictions, though, and individual locations of a chain may not allow dogs even if the rest of the chain does, so you should always call ahead to make sure your Lab will be allowed. Always ask whether there are any pet fees.

Your vacation lodging will be new to your dog, which he may embrace with excitement or may find a little unsettling. Therefore, to avoid any unnecessary anxiety, and prevent disruption such as barking or furniture chewing, he should never be left alone. If your Labrador is crate trained, he may find comfort in sleeping somewhere which is familiar.

When you leave your hotel, you should try to leave it as you found it. The hosts should not have to employ extra cleaning services to return the accommodations to their original state just because your dog was there.

Leaving Your Labrador Retriever at Home

Sometimes you might have to go away and want or need to leave your dog behind. There are plenty of options for you to do this, and there is no particular option which is the "best." Each option will suit certain dogs and families better than others. Also, Labradors in particular are highly adaptable, so this should help take some stress out of the situation.

The first option is to book your Labrador into a boarding kennel. The advantage of these types of establishments is that they are well set up to care for dogs, and the staff are highly experienced in dealing with a variety of different dog personalities, breeds and health issues. This way you can rest assured that professionals are looking after your dog. Boarding kennels are usually well-established businesses within the community, and it will be easy to research reviews on the place to see how previous clients felt they looked after their dogs. You can also visit them prior to going away, to inspect their set-up and get to know the staff. The downside of kennels is that they usually take on a large number of dogs at once, and therefore your dog may have limited one-on-one attention. Dogs usually reside in large runs, with an inside or sheltered section, and an outside section, for the majority of the day, being allowed out once or twice a day to socialize with other dogs and exercise. This might suit your dog brilliantly, but for dogs with a more sensitive nature, they might find it stressful.

Another option is to ask a friend or family member to look after your dog in their own home. This is an excellent option if they already know your dog, as then your dog is familiar with them which may relieve some anxiety in your absence. If your friend or neighbor has other dogs, it is important to make sure the dynamic works before your dog goes to stay with them. Some dogs are highly territorial in their own space, and even if they are best of friends out on a walk, you should not assume that will be the case in their own home. So, ensure you bring your dog over to your friend or family member's house beforehand to gauge how it will go. Remember, your friend or family member is probably doing this for you as a favor, so try to make sure it is as easy for them as possible; stock up with plenty of dog food, chronic medications (if necessary) and all your dog's home comforts, such as bedding and toys.

Finally, the last option is to have a professional pet sitter come and stay in your house. This is a great option for many people, as it means your dog can stay in his own environment, and your house is not being left empty for an extended period of time. Pet sitters are usually experienced at looking after dogs, and therefore, you can rest assured that your dog is getting plenty of attention and being well looked after. If you choose to hire a pet sitter, make sure your dog has had several opportunities to get to know him or her beforehand. You can do this by inviting them over to your house or out on a walk. The downside to pet sitters is that they usually are more expensive than the other options.

***

Whether you're planning on traveling with your Labrador or leaving him at home, a vacation should be relaxing. By taking into account all the aspects discussed in this chapter, you should be able to plan ahead to ensure that your trip is as stress-free as possible for both you and your dog.

CHAPTER 8
Nutrition

"Labrador Retrievers generally have an iron stomach and do well with many diets. I use a premium kibble with a protein source in the first five ingredients. I add carrots, egg, apple slices, blueberries, watermelon, or sweet potato to the kibble to enhance the nutrition. Avoid kibbles that have corn, it's a cheap filler which can cause yeast build up in the ears and cause allergies in the skin. Other grains are good in kibble and are necessary to prevent enlargement of the heart (DCM) from the amino acid Taurine."

Lori Lutz
Bowery Run Labradors

CHAPTER 8   Nutrition

Importance of Nutrition

A balanced diet, appropriate to the life-stage of your Labrador, is one of the most important things that you should provide your dog. Health is closely linked to diet, and if your Labrador is not receiving all the important minerals, vitamins and nutrients that he needs, his underlying health and immunity will suffer.

There are several classes of nutrients which should be taken note of: carbohydrates, proteins, fats, fiber, vitamins and minerals. It is a common misconception that since the ancestors of our dogs were carnivores, domesticated dogs should also eat a predominantly meat-based, high-protein diet. The digestive system of a domesticated dog today is very different from the digestive system of a wolf, and therefore, dogs are now considered omnivorous. That means that even though proteins are essential, dogs also need other non-meat-based ingredients in their diet to make it balanced. All meat, no grain diets have become popular in the dog world recently, however they can actually do more harm than good, resulting in health conditions such as heart and urinary tract diseases. Therefore, balanced diets are essential for keeping your Labrador healthy.

Photo Courtesy of Tim Choldas

A balanced diet will mean a different thing for a puppy compared to an adult Labrador, and therefore feeding a food which is balanced for the life-stage of your Labrador is essential. The American Association of Food Control Officials (AAFCO) sets guidelines for food manufacturing companies, so that they consistently formulate foods which are perfect for puppies, low-energy adults, high-energy adults and seniors. This is one of the benefits of feeding your dog a commercial food. All commercial foods are regulated, and therefore you can be confident that the meal you are providing for your dog, will enable him to obtain all the nutrients that he needs.

Finding a dog food which suits a Labrador is not usually difficult, as Labradors have a raving appetite and will eat almost anything. Therefore, palatability is not usually something that you will need to factor in. However, active working Labradors, senior Labradors and Labradors with joint issues, as discussed in Chapter 12, will all require additional nutrients in their diet to help protect their joints. These include omega-3, omega-6, glucosamine and chondroitin, and are discussed later in this chapter.

Commercial Food

HELPFUL TIP
Obesity

Nearly half of all dogs in the United States are overweight or obese, and dogs can suffer many of the same weight-related health problems as people. Labs, with their oversized appetite, are especially prone to weight problems. People tend to think Labs are supposed to be barrel-chested. You should be able to feel your dog's ribs but not see them. If you can't feel your Lab's ribs, it's time for a diet.

Commercial food can come in a variety of forms such as wet canned food, stew-like food and dry kibble. The best type for your dog is dry food, as it helps keep the teeth clean. As your Labrador bites through the kibble, it provides abrasion to remove some of the tartar which accumulates on the teeth. This helps to reduce the chances of dental disease in the future.

Not all dry food is good quality though. Some manufacturers of cheaper quality dry food will include many bulking ingredients, which can make your Lab feel bloated and full. It can also interfere with house training your Labrador puppy, as after he eats his dinner, the food will swell and make him feel as if he needs to go potty in the middle of the night. One good way to assess the quality of the dry food is to add a cup of water to a cup of dry food and leave overnight. It should swell slightly but not excessively.

When faced with all the choices of commercial food in the stores, you may feel overwhelmed. Most pet stores and veterinary practices have assistants who are trained in canine nutrition and who will be able to help you pick out a suitable food for your Labrador. You should remember that there is no "perfect" choice, and the most important thing is to find a food which suits your Lab. You can do this by first deciding what life-stage your Labrador is at (for example puppy, junior adult, adult, senior adult) and whether he has any additional requirements (for example health conditions, very energetic, working dog). Once you've narrowed down your choice, choose a few products based on their ingredients, discussed further on in this chapter, and look into the customer reviews. This often gives a good insight into whether other people's dogs like the food and do well on it.

CHAPTER 8   Nutrition

Pet Food Labels

"I do not recommend grain free diets as there is some new information that is linking those diets to high incidence of heart disease. Additionally some Labradors have a problem with copper storage and so a low copper kibble is recommended."

Tiffany Ginkel
Cedar Ranch Labrador Retrievers

Pet food labels can tell you a lot about the content of the food. However, if you don't know what you're looking for, or how to compare a label on one type of food to another type of food (for example dry kibble labels to canned food labels), they can seem daunting and fairly useless.

The first part of a pet food label you should look at is the ingredients. The ingredients list is compiled in order of weight. Therefore, the top ingredient is what the product contains the most of. Ideally the top ingredient should be an animal-based protein, such as chicken or beef. More obscure proteins are also used, and these have many benefits for different conditions. For example, turkey, duck or venison are excellent for dogs with allergies, fish is excellent for skin health and joint health, and lamb is great for

Photo Courtesy of
Brittany Pescara
Black Swamp Labradors

picky dogs who need something highly palatable. Meal, for example chicken meal, is dehydrated meat protein, which means that its natural weight is at least 300% more than the ingredient weight, and therefore it's okay if these sorts of proteins are further down the ingredients list. You should never buy a dog food which labels the meat content as "animal-based protein," as this means it is of a lower quality, and the type of protein will vary from batch to batch depending on what is available as off-cuts.

Grains and starchy ingredients are likely to make up the bulk of the rest of the diet. Examples include rice, maize, oats, potato and sweet potato. Some foods pride themselves in being grain-free, which helps dogs with sensitive digestive tracts or skin allergies. However, these diets are often low in taurine, an essential amino acid, a deficiency of which can trigger heart problems such as dilated cardiomyopathy. Therefore, if you choose a grain-free diet, investigate whether additional taurine has been added. If you do choose a diet with grains, whole grains such as brown rice, oats and barley are healthier and provide more fiber than white rice and maize.

Vegetables and possibly fruits, such as pumpkin, peas, carrots, blueberries, cranberries, beet pulp, tomato pomace and alfalfa, are popular ingredients which make up most of the rest of the recipe. These provide essential minerals, vitamins and fiber, which the proteins and carbohydrates may not have provided alone. At the same point in the ingredient list as the vegetables, additional oils might be listed, which help to provide a suitable healthy fat content which includes omega-3 and omega-6. Popular oils include sunflower oil, fish oil, hemp oil and seed oil (such as flaxseed and linseed).

At the bottom of the ingredients list, there may be several ingredients that sounds relatively chemical-like. These ingredients are simply minerals and vitamins to balance the diet, as well as any additional supplements which the food company might decide to put in, such as pre- and probiotics, glucosamine and chondroitin.

Some pet food manufacturers may add coloring to their product. There is no benefit to the dog in the addition of artificial color, and in fact some unnecessary additives can cause health issues so should be avoided.

After looking at the ingredients list, and deciding you are happy that the ingredients look reliably sourced and includes a variety of meats, oils, carbohydrates and vegetables, then you should next look at the guaranteed analysis. This details the percentage of carbohydrates, proteins, fat, fiber, ash and moisture in the diet. These details are per gram of ready-to-eat food, and therefore cannot be directly compared without first doing some calculations.

For example, if a wet food is 75% wet, then it means the dry content is 25%. If the protein level is then 5%, this can be converted by dividing by the dry matter percentage: 5/0.25 = 20% protein on a dry matter basis. Then if a similar dry food, which you wanted to compare, had a moisture content of 10% and a dry content of 90%, with a protein level of 20%, the calculation would be as follows: 20/0.9 = 22.2% protein on a dry matter basis.

Once you have converted your guaranteed analysis into some figures which can be compared, you should choose a food which is high in protein. Ideally this should be over 25% on a dry matter basis, but the higher the better. Fat content should be between 8-12% on a dry matter basis, or even lower if your Labrador needs to lose some weight, and if you are concerned about your Labrador's constant hunger levels, a fiber content above 3% will help him feel fuller for longer.

BARF and Homemade Diets

If you've done any research into diets for dogs, or you've bought your Labrador from a particularly traditional breeder, it is likely that you have come across the concept of BARF or homemade diets. BARF is an acronym which is used to describe "bones and raw food" or "biologically appropriate raw food." The difference between BARF diets and homemade diets is simply whether or not the food is cooked.

BARF and homemade diets have taken the world by storm. Some believe that commercial foods undergo too much processing to be healthy, and therefore a diet made of locally sourced fresh produce will be more nutritious. It also promotes the belief that the ancestors of dogs were primarily meat eaters, and therefore our domesticated dogs should follow this same diet. It doesn't, however, take into consideration that today's domestic dogs are vastly different from their wolf ancestors, and that includes their digestive system.

While there are certainly many benefits of a homemade or BARF diet, including knowing where the ingredients are sourced, knowing that they are organic and free from chemicals, and knowing that minimal processing has been used to make the food, there are also several downsides. The major problem with BARF and homemade diets is the inability to adequately balance them. It is extremely difficult to ensure that there are the right amount of nutrients, minerals and vitamins in a homemade food, which can have an impact on the health of your Labrador. Growing dogs may develop brittle bones, and adult dogs can develop bladder stones and malnutrition.

CHAPTER 8   Nutrition

It isn't impossible to balance a homemade or BARF diet, but it should be done with the aid of a veterinary nutritionist and will probably require the addition of mineral supplements.

Another problem with BARF diets in particular is hygiene. Raw meat can contain bacteria such as salmonella and E. coli, which remains in the mouth of your dog. While your dog's digestive system can deal with these bacteria, they may make vulnerable people in your household ill, such as elderly or young people. The bacteria will be transmitted to the coat of your dog when he grooms himself, and easily picked up if someone pets your Labrador. Therefore, strict hygiene for all household members should apply, which includes regularly washing hands, washing dog food bowls in hot, soapy water after meals, and disinfecting preparation surfaces after use.

Finally, BARF and homemade diets sometimes contain bones. If raw, these bones are usually flexible and dissolve relatively easily in stomach acid. However, it is not always the case. Therefore, any dog on a diet which includes bones has an increased risk of gastrointestinal perforation or blockage, especially Labradors, who rarely chew their food properly!

While BARF and homemade diets can be excellent choices, they are easy to get wrong, and therefore if this is an avenue you would like to explore with your Lab, then it is best to seek advice from a veterinary nutritionist to create a balanced diet for your dog.

Weight Monitoring

As a breed, Labradors have one of the slowest metabolisms, and therefore are prone to obesity. Watching your dog's weight is vital, as excess weight puts strain on the joints, heart, and internal organs, significantly reducing your Lab's life expectancy and ability to exercise comfortably.

There is no "ideal" weight for a Labrador. As mentioned in Chapter 1, males are usually 65–80 lb (29–36 kg) and females are usually 55–70 lb (25–32 kg), but there is a wide genetic variation. Therefore, one Labrador could be underweight at 70 lb and another could be morbidly obese. A better way of assessing your Labrador's weight is by regularly body condition scoring him. An ideal body condition score is 4 to 5, and the range goes from 1 (emaciated) to 9 (obese). The scores are standardized for anybody to use, and are easy and repeatable from dog to dog. These are the descriptions of the following scores:

BCS 1 = Emaciated. Ribs, lumbar vertebral projections, and bony prominences around the pelvis are clearly visible. There is severe loss of muscle and no body fat.

BCS 3 = Underweight. Ribs can be felt with ease and might be visible. Not much fat present. The abdomen tucks up at the flank and a waist can be seen from the top. Some bony projections can be seen. Easy to see top of lumbar vertebrae.

BCS 5 = Ideal. Minimal fat over the ribs and can easily feel them. Waist and ribs are visible when standing above the dog. Tucked abdomen when viewed from the side.

BCS 7 = Overweight. Fat present over ribs and need some pressure to feel them. Fat deposits over rump and around tail base. Cannot easily view waist. Abdominal tuck present but slight.

BCS 9 = Obese. Lots of fat around the base of tail, spine and chest. Abdomen may bulge behind the ribs. No waist or abdominal tuck. Fat deposits on neck and limbs.

Each body condition score is the equivalent of 10% bodyweight. So, for example, if your dog's body condition score is seven, he needs to lose 20% of his bodyweight to reach a healthy score of five. This can then be used to calculate what your dog should weigh. So, if your dog weighs 75 lb, and is 20% overweight, he should actually weigh 60 lb. This is best achieved by feeding the correct amount of food required for his ideal weight, and not his current weight, as directed by the information on the packaging of the food.

However, losing weight is a marathon and not a race, as rapid weight loss can also lead to complications, and therefore, a reduction in weight over approximately six months is a suitable timeline to aim for. Remember, treats also count as calories, and these should be taken into consideration when measuring out the daily amount of food. If you think your dog needs to lose weight, it is always best done by formulating a plan with your veterinarian, and taking him into the veterinary practice for regular weigh-ins.

Food Supplements

You may consider the use of supplements for your Labrador; however, they are unnecessary unless your dog has a problem or has an increased amount of strain on his body, for example as a very active dog.

Food supplements could include probiotics, joint supplements such as glucosamine and chondroitin, skin supplements such as omega oils and biotin, and calming supplements such as L-tryptophan. Some dog foods already have these added to them, so check your Labrador's food before potentially double dosing him.

You can buy supplements from your local vet, pet store or online, and many of them are similar to human versions. However, it is important not to give your Labrador a human health supplement, as human supplements can have additional ingredients to improve taste that may be toxic to your Lab. Supplements usually come in the form of powders, liquids, treats, or tablets, all of which are highly palatable to dogs.

Supplements are generally natural and safe, however you should still discuss the addition of a supplement to your dog's diet with your vet, as occasionally there can be cross reactions with certain medications. However, in general, supplements can be wonderful additions to help keep your Labrador in top condition alongside a balanced, nutritious diet.

CHAPTER 9
Dental Care

Importance of Dental Care

If you've had a Labrador for a while, you may well have gotten used to his doggy odor. However, no matter how much you are nose-blind to the odor of his coat, you will certainly notice when he has bad breath. Bad breath is called halitosis, and is a result of bacteria in the mouth. This can be on the teeth or in the saliva. Routine daily dental care is vital to prevent these bacteria from causing a build-up of plaque and tartar, which can result in swelling of the gums, known as gingivitis, and wobbly and rotten teeth.

Dental disease often goes unnoticed in dogs until it is too late and already causing your dog significant pain. It can silently impact your dog's welfare, and should be prevented at all costs. Most owners assume that their dog will not eat if their mouth is painful, but in the case of a Labrador, their ravenous appetite means they tend to eat regardless of how bad their teeth are. Therefore, it is important to regularly check the mouth of your Lab and provide preventative dental care, to avoid drastic dental work.

CHAPTER 9   Dental Care

Dental Anatomy

A tooth is a bony structure made up of a crown above the gums and a root or roots below the gums. There are 28 deciduous (puppy) teeth which appear within the first few months of life. These fall out, and are replaced by 42 adult teeth between the ages of four and eight months. This is why puppies tend to chew on everything, because the process of teething can be itchy and uncomfortable.

The small teeth at the front of the mouth are called incisors. These would have been used by dogs' wild ancestors to nibble meat off the bone. Next to the incisors are long canines, used for grabbing hold of prey in the wild. Inside a dog's cheeks are bigger flatter teeth called the premolars and molars. These are used to grind harder food.

The outer layer of a tooth is enamel, which is a protective layer. Inside the middle of the tooth is the pulp, which is a fleshy section made up of nerves and blood vessels. This supplies the tooth with all the nutrients needed to survive, and if it becomes exposed, it can cause considerable pain. Around the root of the tooth is the tooth socket. This is a dip in the jaw where the tooth sits. Holding the tooth in the socket is a tough structure called the periodontal ligament. Dental disease weakens this ligament, leading to the tooth becoming wobbly and eventually falling out.

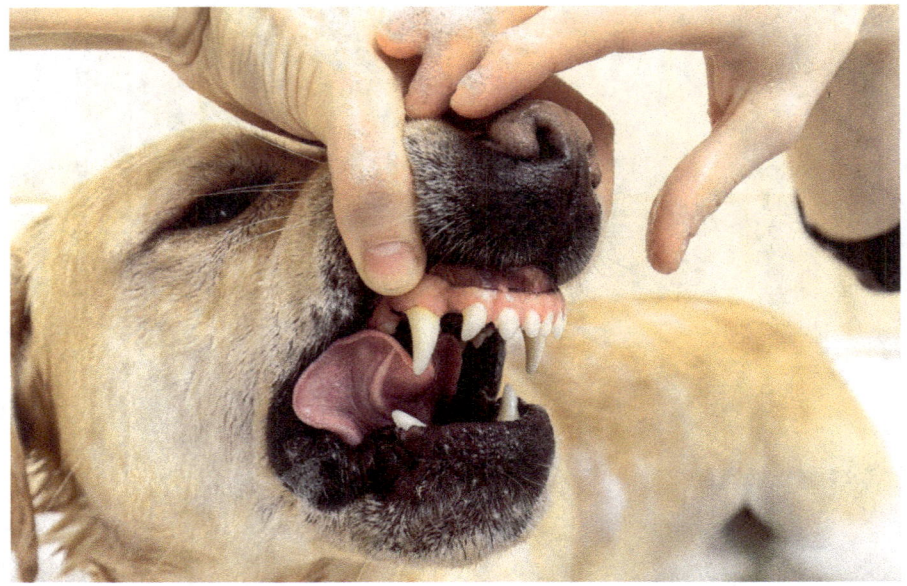

Tartar Build-Up and Gingivitis

Tartar is a mixture of left-over food and bacteria which builds up on the base of the crown. The body reacts to the bacteria by sending inflammatory cells to the area to fight the bacteria, but this just causes the gums to become inflamed and painful. Without removing the tartar, the inflammation, known as gingivitis, becomes worse and worse.

Preventing tartar build-up via dental care and tooth brushing will help prevent gingivitis. If the problem has become severe, or the tartar has become mineralized (known as calculus), it is impossible to remove it without a dental procedure, which is discussed later in the chapter.

Epulis

Labradors are prone to developing a benign tumor of the mouth known as an epulis. The tumor is an overgrowth of gum tissue, usually triggered by chronic inflammation. There are three different types of epulis:

1. Ossifying – a tumor containing a mixture of bone and gum cells.
2. Fibromatous – a tumor made out of tough fibers.
3. Acanthomatous – a destructive type of tumor, which will destroy surrounding tissue including bones.

While epulis aren't technically cancerous and won't spread around the body, they can cause local problems such as bleeding, discomfort and catching food, leading to infections or abscesses. If they are causing problems, they need to be surgically removed, however it is possible for them to regrow afterwards if they cannot be completely excised.

HELPFUL TIP
Puzzle Toys

Puzzle toys are a great way to help your Labrador get physical and mental exercise. They come in a variety of different styles and difficulty levels. Puzzle toys are also a great way to feed your Lab slowly to avoid bloat and prevent begging.

Dental Care

Dental care should start when your dog is a puppy. If you only start once there is dental disease, it is impossible to undo the damage already done. Brushing teeth is not something many dogs will tolerate if it's introduced at an older age, so teaching your Labrador puppy that dental care is a fun and positive experience from a young age will reap its rewards later in life.

The mainstay of dental care is teeth brushing. This helps to remove the build-up of tartar if regularly performed. You should brush your dog's teeth daily if possible, or at least three times a week to be effective. A normal or children's toothbrush can be used, however you might find it easier to use a finger brush, which is a plastic thimble-like item with bristles which you insert over your finger, or an angled dog toothbrush to help get to the back of the mouth. You should never use human toothpaste, as it is toxic to dogs. Dog toothpaste is available from many pet stores, vets and online, and is formulated using enzymes to break down the tartar, kill bacteria, and freshen breath.

When brushing the teeth, it is easy to miss the molars right at the back, so ensure you pull your Labrador's big jowls back to reach them. When you are done with brushing, give him plenty of fuss and rewards to make it a positive experience for him.

Dental brushing can be complemented with the use of dental chews. They are not a replacement for brushing, but can be useful to make sure the teeth are clean in between times, as long as your Labrador actually chews them and doesn't swallow them at lightning speed with minimal chewing! The concept behind dental chews is that they are shaped so that they cause

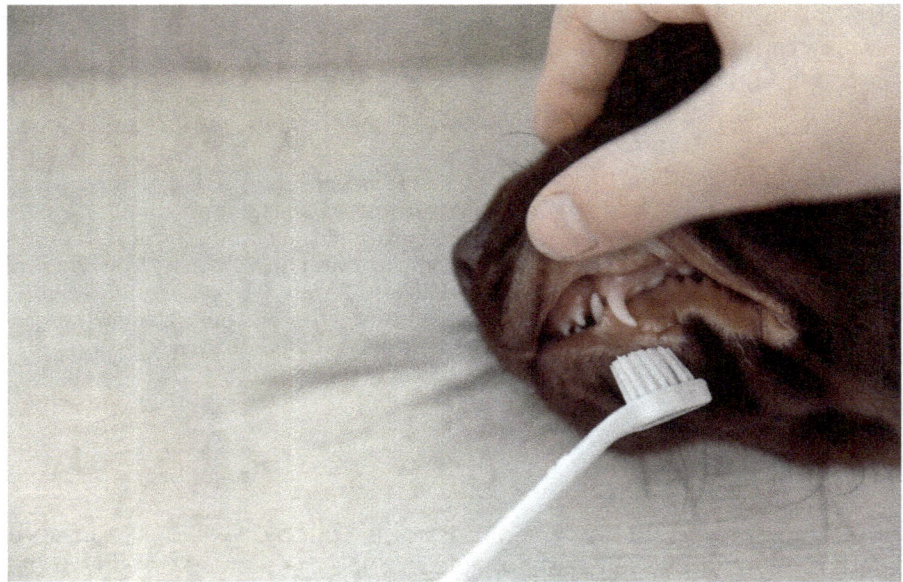

friction, abrasion or suction to the tooth, so that tartar which has not become too adhered yet comes off. Don't forget treats contain calories though, and all Lab owners need to watch their dog's waistline, so remember to remove the equivalent number of calories out of your dog's normal food.

Another option for keeping teeth clean is canine dental wash. This can be added to drinking water and works in a similar manner to toothpaste, as it has enzymes in it to help dissolve off tartar. It will also help to freshen breath. However, if the tartar has already built up for a while, it will make no difference. Just as with toothpaste, you should always use mouthwash formulated specifically for dogs. Human mouthwash is toxic to dogs and can cause serious consequences.

You can use a variety of dental care products to look after your Labrador's teeth, however the most effective way of managing your dog's teeth is by feeding dry food. Dry dog kibble, like dental chews, helps to remove tartar as your dog chews through it. The kibble size should be as large as possible for a medium-large sized dog, or even better, should be specialist dental food. This food is large sized kibble that creates a slight suction when teeth chew through it, resulting in more removal of tartar.

CHAPTER 9   Dental Care

Dental Procedures

If your dog has dental disease, or tartar build-up which is not improving with diligent dental care, he may need a dental procedure. This is a procedure which your vet will do for you, and afterwards, your Lab's teeth will look like he is a puppy again.

A dental procedure, which can be performed at your local vet practice, requires a general anesthetic; however, your Labrador will only need to be at the vet clinic for the day, and will be ready to go home in the afternoon once he's woken up. The procedure will start by scaling off all the tartar from the teeth to decrease the bacterial burden in the mouth. After that, the vet will probe around every tooth to investigate whether any need to be removed. If they do, he will loosen the periodontal ligament with a special tool called an elevator to be able to extract the tooth. If the socket is large, your vet might choose to suture it closed to prevent food from packing into it. After this, the remaining teeth will be polished, and the mouth rinsed out.

Your Labrador will probably come home with antibiotics and pain relief if he has had teeth removed, and may feel a bit under the weather during the evening, however he should feel back to his normal self by the next morning.

Even though it might seem invasive to book your dog in for a dental procedure, he will feel so much better afterwards, with a pain-free mouth, and you will enjoy having a Labrador with fresh breath!

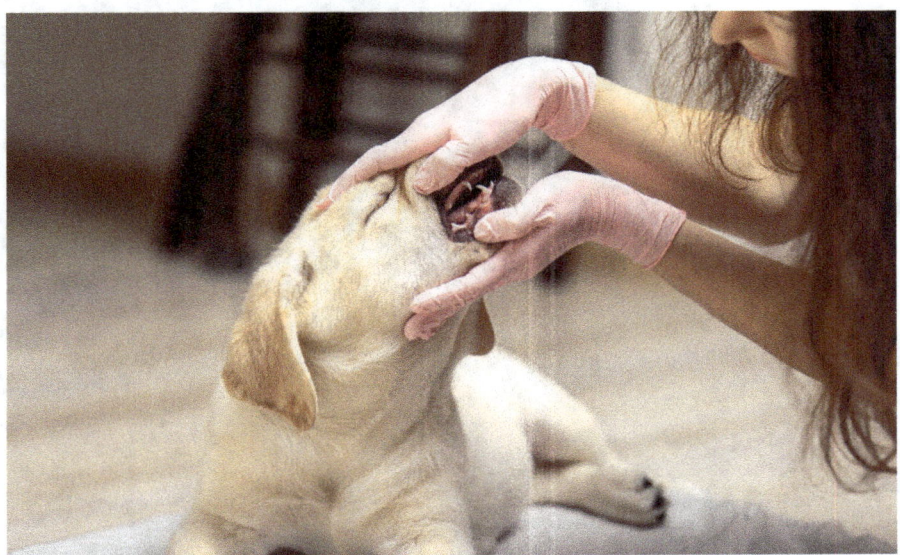

CHAPTER 10
Grooming

Grooming a Labrador should not be a difficult task if you have trained your Labrador to accept being groomed from the age of a puppy. It's important that Labradors learn to tolerate all aspects of grooming, including bathing, brushing and ear cleaning, as since they are naturally attracted to swimming, they may need a bath or ear clean more often than the average dog. In addition, Labradors are moderate to heavy shedders, especially twice a year, and therefore grooming your dog will help reduce hair in your house.

Photo Courtesy of Tom Powell

CHAPTER 10 Grooming

About the Coat

"They shed about four times a year, where they lose lots of their undercoat. But they also do lose some fur daily. Brushing weekly will help cut down on the hair pileups. My best advice: choose a Lab whose coat color goes with your home and clothes!"

Jennifer Robinson
Chestnut's Labs2Love

As discussed in Chapter 1, Labradors have a dense, water-repellent double coat which sheds heavily twice a year in spring and fall. This was developed so that when the original Labradors were working in the icy Canadian waters, they would be protected from the chill of the water. They were preferred over longhaired Retrievers, as the ice could encrust on the longhaired Retrievers' coat, resulting in them taking longer to warm up.

A 'double-coat' means that there are two layers of fur. The 'guard coat' or 'top coat' has a coarser feel to it, and the 'under coat' is softer and fairer, with natural water repellent oil secretions. Combined together, it makes it very difficult for water to contact the skin directly, and serves as an excellent insulator.

Luckily, even though the coat is thick, it is relatively short and sleek, and therefore not difficult to care for. Double-coated dogs should never be shaved, which means that you probably won't need to take your Labrador to the groomer's to be maintained.

> **HELPFUL TIP**
> **Labs Shed – A LOT!**
>
> Many people seem to think that short-haired dogs like Labs don't shed. In fact, Labs shed a lot all year round instead of just during the changing of the seasons. Deshedding tools will come in handy. You should NEVER shave a Lab. Not only will it still shed, but now you've created hair splinters that are harder to remove from furniture and carpet. It can also destroy your Lab's coat and lead to sunburn and overheating.

Coat Health

"Labrador Retrievers are generally very low maintenance for their coats. A good brush to buy is the 'Furminator' and a good shampoo to have on hand is 'Curaseb* in case of hot spots in summer or bacterial/yeast problem developing in the coat."

Lori Lutz
Bowery Run Labradors

Keeping your Labrador's coat healthy will require frequent brushing and occasional bathing.

You should groom your Labrador as frequently as possible, as not only will it help to remove loose hairs and therefore reduce shedding, it will improve the circulation to the skin to help the health and shine of the coat,

---

* *Curaseb should only be used to treat medical conditions and not as a general use shampoo*

CHAPTER 10 Grooming

and regular grooming will help you spot problems early. It will also improve your bond with your dog. If you can brush your dog daily, this is excellent, however once or twice a week is sufficient.

You only need a few types of brushes to brush your Labrador:

- A pin brush, with long metal bristles
- A bristle brush, with soft tightly packed bristles
- Optional extras: a slicker brush (like a pin brush with shorter metal bristles) and a greyhound comb (a metal comb for longer hair)

Start by using a pin brush and brush in the direction of the hair with long strokes. Once you've warmed up your Labrador with this, you can use the brush to brush in shorter, brisk strokes, in directions other than the natural flow of the fur. This helps to part the coat and brush a bit deeper down towards the skin. Finally, you can finish brushing with a soft bristle brush to relax your Labrador and encourage the distribution of the natural oils throughout the coat.

Brushing can be preceded by giving your Labrador a bath. However, bathing too frequently with shampoo will strip the natural oils from the coat, reducing the shine and ability to provide a waterproofing layer. Nevertheless, Labradors are a magnet to water and mud, so you may find your Lab needs a bath relatively frequently. To avoid stripping the coat of oils, you can use lukewarm water to rinse out the dirt from the coat, and only use shampoo when your dog is beginning to smell, which should ideally not be more frequent than once a month.

Baths are best done inside in the bath, but on a warm day, you can gently put the outside hose on your Labrador outside instead. You should use lukewarm water, ideally from a detachable showerhead, however if you don't have this option, a cup or a jug can be used to pour the water.

There are many shampoos on the market which can be used on dogs. You should try to pick a dog shampoo which is gentle on the skin, and designed not to dry it out. Oatmeal shampoo is a popular choice for this reason. However, your veterinarian or pet shop assistant will be able to give you advice on the products available for sale.

When bathing your dog, there are places which are easily missed, such as in between the pads under the paws, and cleaning around the eyes and face. It might be easier to address these areas with grooming wipes instead of washing.

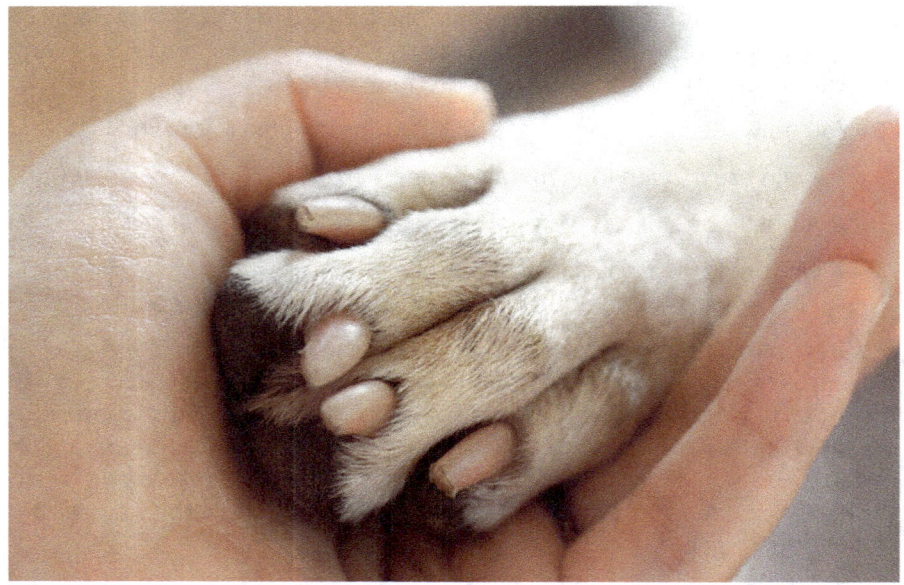

Nail Clipping

Nail clipping is really important if you don't regularly walk your dog on hard ground. This is because he will not have a way of naturally filing his nails, and therefore they might grow excessively and in-grow into the paws, resulting in extreme pain.

The nails are made of keratin, and if cut correctly, the cutting process does not cause any pain. However, the center of the nail is called the quick, and is full of blood vessels and nerves. If this is accidentally cut, it can bleed profusely and be very painful. It is important to teach your Labrador to stay still when cutting the nails, to reduce the chances of this happening. Start when your Labrador is a puppy, by regularly touching his paws, picking them up, and touching his nails. This will get him used to the process before you cut the nails for the first time.

To cut your Labrador's nails, you will want to purchase a large nail clipper from your local pet store. A large one will be needed because an adult Labrador has thick and tough nails. When you clip your dog's nails, start by just clipping a small amount away to avoid cutting into the quick. You might be lucky and have a Labrador with clear nails, and therefore you can see the quick, but most Labradors will have black nails, which makes it very difficult. Sometimes if you turn the paw upside down, you can see where the quick extends to, but this is not the case for all dogs. So, if you are not confident

CHAPTER 10 Grooming

about cutting your Labrador's nails, you can ask your veterinarian, veterinary nurse or local dog groomer to help you.

If you do accidentally cut the quick, the important thing is not to panic. Place some pressure on the bleeding paw with a wad of cotton wool, or if you have a silver nitrate coagulation pen (also available from your local pet store or online), you can hold this on the area which is bleeding for a few seconds to stem the blood flow.

Some dogs that are phobic about nail clippers may tolerate a nail grinder or Dremel. This is a rechargeable tool that files the nail rather than cuts it.

Ear Cleaning

"Since Labrador Retrievers have ear flaps (ears that fold over the ear canal) it is important to check for debris and use a high quality ear wash if any odor is detected."

Lori Lutz
Bowery Run Labradors

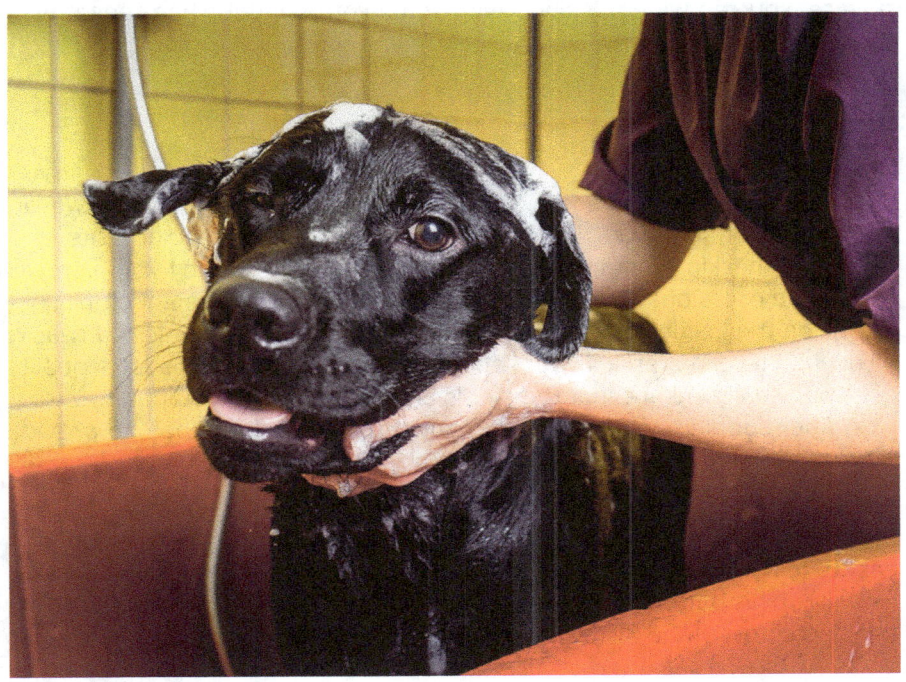

111

Labradors are prone to ear infections due to the conformation of their ears. Since the pinna (flap) of the ear folds down over the opening of the ear, it creates a moist environment ideal for bacteria and yeast to grow. In addition to this, repeatedly getting wet when swimming, particularly in dirty water, provides a perfect environment for infections.

Nevertheless, if you clean your dog's ears regularly, he will have a much better chance of staying infection-free, as the aim of ear cleaners is not only to clean the ear through dissolving wax and removing dirt, but they also change the environment inside the ear to one which is not favored by bacteria and yeasts. You can clean your Labrador's ears after every time he has been swimming, or simply routinely once a month if he has no problems, or once every one to two weeks if he has recurrent infections. Ear cleaner can be purchased from a pet store, online or at a veterinary practice, but the best ones are veterinary approved, so it is worth inquiring which one your veterinarian recommends.

Start by holding up the flap of your dog's ear, then placing the nozzle into the ear canal and giving a squirt. When you have put a sufficient amount in, place the ear flap back down, and massage the whole area for 20-30 seconds. Your dog will then likely shake his head when you let go, but this is a good thing, as it brings all the loosened wax and dirt to the surface. You can wipe this away with some cotton wool. Then repeat with the other ear.

Anal Glands

Most groomers will empty your dog's anal glands for you. However, you might not send your Labrador to the groomer for regular visits, and therefore checking them and emptying them yourself, or by your vet, will be needed occasionally. The anal glands sit at the four and eight o'clock positions on the inside of the anus. They are redundant sacs which can easily fill up with fecal material if your Lab's stools are looser than usual. A quality diet will usually ensure that the stools are normal, but if you find he struggles, fiber supplements in the diet can help firm up the stools to provide more stimulation as the stools pass.

When the anal sacs become filled, they will need to be emptied by a vet, veterinary nurse, or groomer, to ensure they do not become infected. It is easy to tell if they are full because your Labrador will definitely let you know. He will rub his bottom along the ground, known as scooting, to try to relieve the discomfort of the filled sacs. He is also likely to lick the area. If you miss those clues, you certainly won't miss the repugnant fishy odor that filled anal glands bring into your house!

If your dog has recurrent issues with his anal glands, they can be removed, however it can be a risky procedure as the nerves to the anal sphincter run just behind them. If damaged, the anal sphincter can become leaky, which is unhygienic for your dog and the house. Before surgery, your vet may try routine emptying of the glands every two weeks, or flushing them under anesthetic.

***

Keeping your Labrador well-groomed is not too challenging compared to long-coated breeds of dogs, but nevertheless it shouldn't be neglected. Your Labrador will thrive on the extra attention, and not only will it improve his health, but it will improve your bond too.

CHAPTER 11
Preventative Veterinary Medicine

"Environment plays a role in longevity of the lives of our dogs as much as genetics can. Obesity can cause hip dysplasia in a dog from a genetically sound pairing and cancer can be caused from diet and exposure to lawn chemicals in an otherwise genetically strong line. Genetics is only 50% of the equation which can be reduced by purchasing from a breeder who health tests their breeding pair and can trace it multiple generations back on both sides of the parents. The other 50% is managed by the owner who provides proper diet, exercise, and exposure to the outside world."

Lori Lutz
Bowery Run Labradors

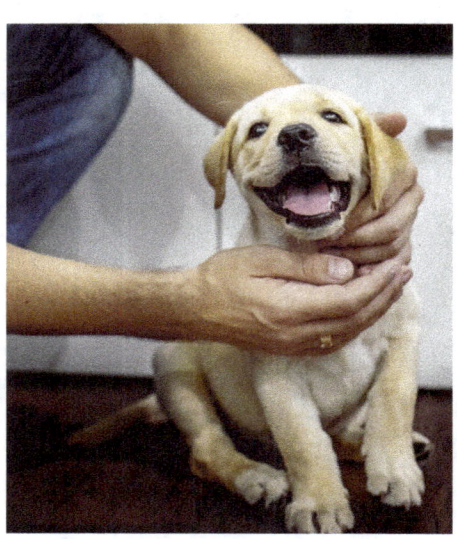

Naturally, your main concern for your Labrador is keeping him healthy. Your veterinarian can help with this, and is not only available to help treat health problems, but also to help prevent them. After all, prevention is better than cure. With the Labrador's long list of potential health issues, as further discussed in Chapter 12, it is worth choosing a veterinarian who you fully trust and that can get to know your Labrador like his own. This way, he can help you to prevent potential problems and keep your Labrador healthy.

CHAPTER 11   Preventative Veterinary Medicine

Choosing a Veterinarian

There are many aspects which you will need to consider when choosing a veterinarian. It is in your Labrador's best interests for you to stick to a single veterinarian or veterinary practice, to make sure the vet is kept up to date about your Labrador's health. Also, should you need to make a pet insurance claim (later discussed in this chapter), it is simpler if your dog's full clinical history is just held at one practice. Therefore, finding a vet who you feel you can trust for the lifetime of your dog should not be taken lightly.

HELPFUL TIP
Parasites

Parasites such as fleas and ticks may seem like just a nuisance, but they can lead to your dog becoming sick. Ticks, in particular, carry a wide variety of diseases including Lyme disease and Rocky Mountain Spotted Fever. And while heartworm prevention may seem like an unnecessary expense, think of it this way: preventing heartworm is significantly cheaper than treating it.

The first consideration is the vet's experience. Some vets have been practicing for decades, whereas others are new to the career. Some will have taken on post-graduate studies, and some practices may even be able to offer vets with specialist services, such as cardiology, ophthalmology and orthopedic training. This is an excellent benefit as it means that if your Labrador has a problem, he doesn't need to travel long distances to a referral hospital. You shouldn't be put off if your potential vet is still relatively newly qualified. What they might lack in experience will be supported by senior staff for second opinions, and often younger vets are more up to date with recent changes in veterinary medicine, in comparison to older vets who might have more practical experience, but are behind on new developments.

The next consideration is the distance from your house. If your Labrador ever needs medical attention in the case of an emergency, every minute could mean life or death to him. While you don't necessarily have to choose the closest vet practice to you, it is a good idea to be able to travel to your vet within 20 minutes if needed.

Another important consideration is whether "extras" are important to you. Some veterinary practices run extra services, such as grooming, boarding, training classes, puppy socialization classes, weight maintenance clinics, diabetic clinics and veterinary nurse consults. It's not essential to have access to all these services at your local veterinary practice, however having them all in one place will help your Labrador feel like he's going somewhere familiar every time.

Emergency services are also an important thing to enquire about. Not all veterinary practices offer an after-hours emergency service, and it is now common for a vet to send after-hours patients to a dedicated emergency service. This does have its benefits, as the vets working at the emergency service are trained specifically in emergency and critical care, and therefore you can rest assured that your Lab is receiving the best treatment. However, the inconvenience of this is that it is often more expensive, and requires

Photo Courtesy of Alli Wright

CHAPTER 11   Preventative Veterinary Medicine

taking your dog back to your normal vet for hospitalization during the day if necessary.

Finally, on most people's mind is finances. In reality, most veterinary practices are relatively competitive on pricing so there should not be a big variation in cost. However, some practices might offer loyalty programs or healthy pet plans which enable you to get a discount off routine procedures such as neutering, vaccinations, parasite treatment and microchipping. These are worth signing up for, as not only do they help you save money, they will also remind you to keep up to date with preventative treatment.

Vaccinations

Vaccinations should form a major part of your Labrador's preventative health measures. There are many deadly diseases in the world which can be easily prevented by vaccinations.

You should begin your Labrador puppy's vaccinations at 8 weeks old, and if the breeder only releases your puppy after this, they should have had their first vaccination when you pick him up. A puppy vaccination course might require two or three vaccines, each two to four weeks apart, depending on the brand of vaccine and disease risk in your geographical area.

After your puppy's primary vaccinations, he should receive a booster at a year old, and then annually after that. Some people choose to perform a blood test to check for immunity levels, and then only vaccinate when immunity levels dip. However, this is not necessary since vaccinations are extremely safe with adverse effects only occurring very rarely.

Vaccines are divided into two categories: core and non-core vaccines. The core vaccines vary depending on the prevalence of diseases in your geographical area, but the common diseases vaccinated against include parvovirus, distemper, hepatitis (canine adenovirus), leptospirosis, parainfluenza, Bordetella and rabies.

Parvovirus is a disease which affects mainly puppies, although dogs of any age can contract it. It is a deadly virus which causes bleeding into the gut, and diarrhea. Some dogs may also vomit. This leads to rapid dehydration. It is picked up mainly through fecal-oral transmission, or sharing of food and water bowls.

Hepatitis, otherwise known as canine adenovirus, is a disease which affects the liver. The inflammation in the liver can cause a fever, vomiting, lethargy, diarrhea, jaundice, enlarged lymph nodes and eventually leads to death.

Distemper is a virus which affects many different body systems. It initially causes vomiting, sneezing and coughing, as well as thickened pads on the paws and the tip of the nose. Once the virus has spread to the brain it causes seizures.

Leptospirosis is a disease which has several different variants, known as serotypes. Some vets vaccinate against the two most common ones, some vaccinate against four. It can cause similar symptoms to hepatitis, such as vomiting, diarrhea and jaundice, but it also will cause neurological symptoms. It mainly affects the kidneys, liver, central nervous system and reproductive system.

Kennel cough is a disease which is vaccinated against by squirting the vaccine up the nose. Kennel cough is actually a complex of diseases, which are commonly caused by Bordetella and parainfluenza in combination. Kennel cough causes a harsh goose-honk or hacking cough, and may cause phlegm to be brought up. It can easily be mistaken for vomiting.

Rabies is the final vaccination which is vital in areas of the world where it is endemic. Rabies is a disease which affects the brain, and is spread through saliva which has contaminated blood. This may be through bites, or simply saliva contaminating a scratch. It is transmissible to humans.

Distemper, hepatitis and parvovirus are often combined into one injectable vaccination, which is sometimes also combined with leptospirosis and possibly parainfluenza in one syringe. If parainfluenza isn't given in the injectable form, it can be combined with Bordetella in a vaccine which squirts up the nose. Rabies, however, is given as an individual injectable vaccination.

Microchipping

A microchip is a rice-sized metal insert which can be inserted into the scruff of your dog's neck via an injection by your veterinarian. It may seem that an injection to insert a microchip will be painful, but the pain is quick, and very short lasting. Most puppies will have forgotten about it within seconds of the injection.

A microchip is a very good idea, as if your Labrador gets lost or stolen, and is subsequently picked up by animal control or taken to a veterinarian, a quick scan of the microchip will enable him to be reunited with you swiftly. In certain parts of the world, such as the UK, microchips are a legal requirement and non-optional.

Needless to say, a microchip is useless if your details are not kept up to date on it. Every time you move house or change your cell number you should contact the microchip database holding company to alter your details. That way you can be confident that your dog can be retraced to you easily.

External Parasites

Fleas present a major threat for the health of your Labrador and are common external parasites. Depending on where you live geographically, mange mites and ticks might also present a threat.

External parasites can be picked up by your Labrador from other animals, from the environment, and even from you bringing them into the house on your clothes. Fleas and mites cause intense itching due to their bites, resulting in being able to observe a red rash and your Labrador scratching. The difference is mites are microscopic, and fleas can be seen by the naked eye. Even so, 95% of fleas live in the environment, which means they are not always obvious on your dog. An easy test to see if your dog has fleas is to rub the coat over a white kitchen paper towel, to remove some

Photo Courtesy of Chris Norton

dirt and dust from the coat. When a small amount of water is dripped on the dirt, if it is flea dirt, it will stain the kitchen paper brown or dark red.

Ticks, on the other hand, don't usually cause discomfort, unless the bite becomes locally infected. The greater concern is that ticks can transmit diseases to your dog, and therefore, should be removed quickly or prevented. It is worth keeping a tick hook to hand, which can be purchased from your vet, the pet store or online. A tick hook enables easy removal of the tick without touching it, and ensures the mouth parts are removed cleanly, as it is when these are left in the skin that infection can occur.

External parasites can be prevented with anti-parasitic treatment. Preventative treatment can last a few weeks to a few months, depending on the product used. It can come in the form of tablets, treats, spot-on pipettes and collars. You can also use anti-parasitic shampoos which kill parasites, but they won't leave a residual protection. Some anti-parasitic treatments can be bought from a pet shop, and others can be bought from a veterinary practice. The veterinary practice products, however, are likely to be prescription strength and therefore have less resistance build-up against the drug. Therefore, they often work better.

CHAPTER 11   Preventative Veterinary Medicine

Internal Parasites

Just as you should routinely treat for external parasites, you should also routinely treat for internal parasites. The most common types of worms include:

- Intestinal roundworms and tapeworms: These cause diarrhea, weight loss and bloating. In extreme cases, they can cause life-threatening gastrointestinal blockages.
- Lungworms: These worms stop blood from being able to clot, and can cause bleeding into the eyes. They also cause a cough, which can lead to respiratory distress since they cause damage to the lungs.
- Heartworms: These reproduce in the circulatory system, and can cause life-threatening blockages in the heart, arteries and small vessels in the lungs and leading to the brain.

Some flea treatments also include worming treatments, so one application of a medication will cover all types of parasites, but you should follow your vet's recommendations about what treatments to use on your dog.

Comprehensive worming treatments against roundworms and tapeworms are usually recommended every three months if your dog scavenges, or every six months if he doesn't. Therefore, for Labradors with ravenous appetites, you will certainly have to worm every three months! If you live in an area where lungworms are prevalent, it is actually best to deworm your dog with a roundworm treatment every month, and then with a tapeworm treatment every three months.

Neutering

If you don't plan to breed your Labrador, which you shouldn't be considering if you are not an experienced breeder, it is in your Labrador's best interests to be neutered. Neutering males prevents unwanted matings, reduce the urge to roam which could lead to traffic accidents, prevent sexual frustration, reduce marking, reduce aggressive tendencies (although the Labrador should not naturally have any aggressive tendencies), reduce prostate conditions and eliminate cancers of the reproductive organs. Spaying a female will eliminate messy times when she is in heat, prevent unwanted pregnancies, reduce and almost eliminate the chances of mammary cancers, prevent uterine and ovarian cancers, and prevent a life-threatening uterine infection called a pyometra.

Both castration and spaying procedures require your dog to be a day patient at your local veterinary practice. He will need to be dropped off early on in the day, having had nothing for breakfast. The operation is usually done in the morning and your dog will usually be discharged in the afternoon, after a few hours of observation. The anesthetic will take the rest of the day to wear off, so don't worry if your Lab seems a little off color. You can give him some plain food, such as chicken and rice, and let him sleep for the rest of the day. By the next day, you should notice a big improvement. In the two weeks following the operation, it is really important that you don't let your Labrador run around too much, jump up or lick at the incision. These can cause the dog's stitches to come out and a wound infection to develop, which will significantly slow the healing and require extra medication. Most vets like to check the incision after two to three days, and then again after 14 days to take out the stitches.

Pet Insurance

When you first buy or rescue a Labrador, you should consider taking out pet insurance. As discussed in Chapter 12, Labradors are prone to many conditions, and having pet insurance will give you peace of mind that the financial burden of these conditions should be covered to a point. Veterinary fees can run into thousands of dollars, quickly and unexpectedly, and many people cannot afford a sudden payment of this size. Pet insurance will therefore give you the opportunity to make decisions about your Labrador's healthcare without the worry of finances.

When deciding on which pet insurer to choose, you should read the fine print carefully. There are several different types of policies. Some give you a pot of money which you can use yearly for any condition, some will give you a smaller pot of money per year per condition, and some will have a maximum that can be spent on a condition for the lifetime of your dog. There's no right or wrong option, but you may find one will suit you over another. For many insurance companies there are also three different levels of coverage, in addition to how the money is divided up:

- Accident coverage
- Accident and illness coverage
- Accident, illness and routine care coverage (which includes contributions towards vaccinations, parasite control, neutering, and dental care)

If you rescue or acquire an older Labrador, you may find that there are some restrictions from the insurance company on your policy. They may place exclusions or request a higher excess payment on each claim. They may even pay out a smaller portion of each claim above the excess amount, and therefore, do not assume the standard policy will be applicable to an older dog. In the same way, if you have had your Labrador from a young age, and only sign him up for insurance when he's older, you are likely to have a worse deal compared to if you had had him on an insurance policy his entire life. This is because the insurance company is taking on more risk, as elderly dogs tend to have more conditions wrong with them.

It is worth insuring your Labrador from the day you bring him home, as any conditions that he sees a vet for will form part of his clinical history, and be excluded from claims in the future. Conversely, if your insurance is already in place when your dog is first treated for a condition, he will be covered for as long as the terms stated in your particular insurance policy. As Labradors can be prone to many expensive lifelong conditions, a life policy is recommended.

You are not alone if you feel that paying pet insurance is like throwing away money, and you might wish to consider opening up special account to put aside money specifically for your Labrador. Unfortunately, it is likely that this sum of money is not going to be enough for what you might actually need if your Labrador suddenly has a major accident or develops a chronic, lifelong illness. Instead, you will probably find that pet insurance would pay for itself over the lifetime of your Lab.

Pet insurance will eliminate much of the worry of providing for your dog, as if something unexpected arises, you know that he will be covered. Therefore, by purchasing pet insurance, and providing the preventative veterinary measures which have been outlined in this chapter, you can ensure that you are giving your dog every opportunity to live a healthy, happy life.

CHAPTER 12
Labrador Retriever Health Conditions

As with most purebred breeds of dog, Labrador Retrievers can be genetically predisposed to developing health conditions. These arise from inbreeding and poor selection of parents by breeders. Most kennel club breeders will aim to breed genetically linked diseases out, through diligent genetic testing and not breeding from any dogs that develop a condition. However, less professional breeders and backyard breeders may be more indiscriminate in their choices of parents, and therefore the offspring may have a higher chance of health problems. As a result, it is worth investing in a puppy from a breeder who is kennel club registered and has a reputation for breeding high quality, healthy puppies.

Cardiac Conditions

Cardiac conditions are health conditions which affect the heart or circulatory system. They can be life-threatening.

Atrioventricular Block

The heart muscle is triggered by electrical impulses to contract and pump the blood out of the heart. This happens in a regular rhythm, produc-

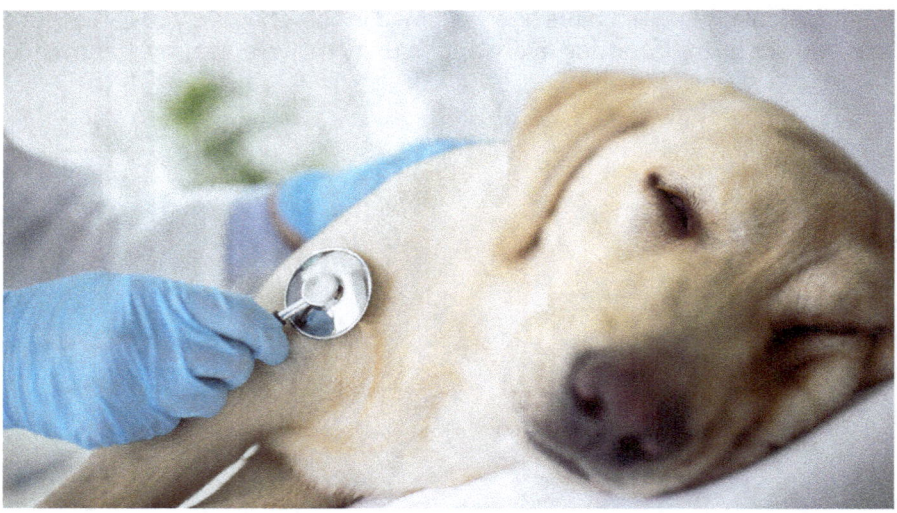

ing a regular beat to the heart. If the rhythm alters, apart from a slight increase in speed when breathing in and decrease in speed when breathing out, this is termed an arrhythmia.

An atrioventricular block is when only the top part of the heart has the electrical signal to beat, and the bottom half doesn't. This causes the heart to miss part of the beat, and is termed an atrioventricular (or AV) block. Sometimes, this can happen intermittently, known as a second-degree AV block, and sometimes it happens with every beat, known as a third-degree AV block.

Symptoms include exercise intolerance, fainting and in serious cases, heart failure.

AV block can be treated with medications to help the heart beat more regularly and effectively, however serious cases may need a pacemaker fitted.

Pericardial Effusion

The pericardium is a sac surrounding the heart. When fluid accumulates inside the pericardial sac, around the heart, it is called a pericardial effusion. Male Labradors are at a higher risk than female Labradors. There can be many reasons for fluid accumulating around the heart, such as primary heart failure, but in Labradors, the main reason seems to be "idiopathic," meaning unknown or no cause.

The symptoms of pericardial effusion are related to the heart having less space to pump, due to restriction from the fluid surrounding it. These include collapse, fluid build-up in the abdomen due to a back-up of blood trying to enter the heart, decreased pulses and weakness.

The fluid can be drained from the pericardial sac by a veterinarian which usually resolves the symptoms unless the underlying cause triggers the fluid to return.

Tricuspid Valve Dysplasia

The tricuspid valve is a valve inside the right side of the heart which prevents backflow of blood when the heart muscle contracts. Tricuspid valve dysplasia is a malformation of the valve, which causes it to be defective. This can lead to the sound of a heart murmur, due to turbulent blood flow within the heart, and right-sided enlargement of the heart due to an overload in blood volume.

Clinical symptoms include fatigue and a fast heart rate, which eventually lead to heart failure symptoms such as abdominal fluid accumulation (known as ascites) and fluid on the lungs.

The prognosis is dependent on the severity of the dysplasia, however if only mild, it can be managed with medication which improves the pumping efficacy of the heart and reduces fluid build-up in the lungs and abdomen.

Dermatological Conditions

Dermatological conditions are conditions of the skin. While they are not life-threatening, they can cause significant discomfort.

Atopic Dermatitis

Atopic dermatitis, also known as skin allergies, manifests in several different ways. The most common way is itchy skin, usually in the belly, groin, armpit and paw regions. The ear canals also can become inflamed and in more rare cases the bowel can become upset too, leading to diarrhea. There doesn't appear to be a pattern between the different allergens and different areas which become inflamed on the body, but rather it varies on each individual basis. Allergens can include food proteins (such as chicken, beef, etc.), environmental allergens (such as grass, pollen, etc.) and insect allergies (such as mites, fleas, etc.).

It is uncommon that a dog is just allergic to one thing, and usually several allergens are involved. Discovering which are the culprits is a process of elimination. There is the option for blood tests to be performed to investigate the reaction to different allergens, however these tests can be expensive as well as non-specific and inconclusive in their results. Nevertheless, in some cases, the results can be helpful for allergen avoidance or creation of a vaccination against the allergies.

Apart from the development of allergen vaccines, there are several treatment options for managing allergies. These are aimed at reducing inflammation in the skin or reducing the immune response, and include steroids, antihistamines and immunosuppressants. There are also ways of managing the skin so that the skin barrier is in better health and doesn't become as inflamed. These include the addition of omega oils to the diet, which are natural anti-inflammatories and improve the health of the skin barrier, and soothing shampoos, such as oatmeal shampoo.

Unfortunately, atopic dermatitis is a lifelong condition, so it is important to find the most effective way to manage it for your Labrador.

CHAPTER 12   Labrador Retriever Health Conditions

Endocrine Conditions

Endocrine conditions are conditions of organs or glands which produce and secrete hormone messengers into the blood, which regulate metabolism, growth, tissue function, sleep, mood and reproduction.

Diabetes Mellitus

Diabetes mellitus is a condition which is more common in neutered Labradors, compared to ones which have not been castrated or spayed. This is the opposite compared to other breeds, where spaying females actually reduces the chances of diabetes.

Diabetes is a condition where either insulin is not produced, or the body's cells do not respond to insulin, resulting in a high blood glucose (sugar) level. A high blood sugar level can cause symptoms such as increased thirst, increased urination, a change in hunger levels (which are usually initially increased, then progress to decreased), cataracts, weight loss and weakness. If left untreated, diabetes is life-threatening.

Diabetes is treated with insulin injections, which are administered in the scruff of the neck. Only very small amounts of insulin are needed, and the needles are tiny, meaning your Labrador probably won't even notice. The injections are administered twice a day, 12 hours apart, after a meal. Initially frequent monitoring of glucose levels by your vet will be needed to be able to adjust the insulin injections to the ideal amount, but once the ideal volume of insulin has been discovered, the prognosis is good with diligent treatment.

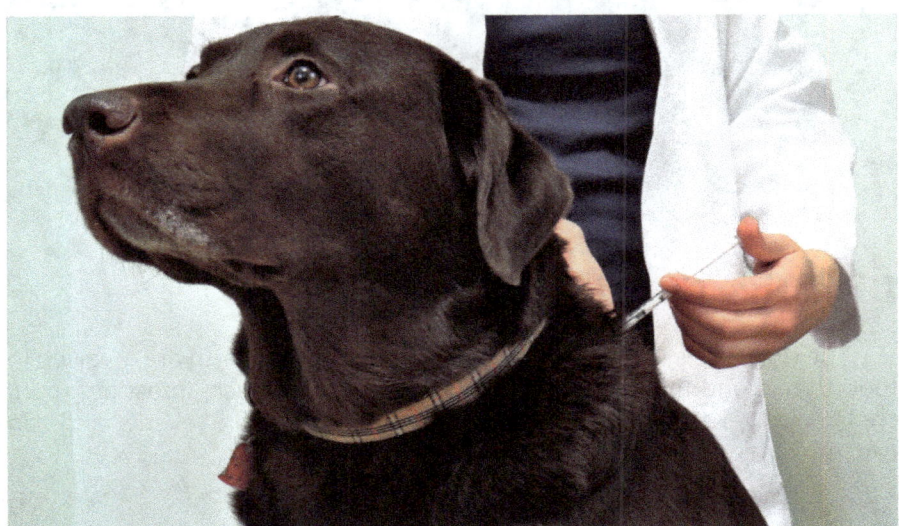

Hypothyroidism

The thyroid gland produces thyroid hormones which control the body's metabolism. Most cases of hypothyroidism develop from the destruction of the thyroid gland, and therefore an inability to produce thyroid hormones.

It might be difficult to spot whether your dog has hypothyroidism, as clinical symptoms can be nonspecific. Common signs include an increase in weight without an increase in appetite, mental dullness, lethargy or unwillingness to exercise, seeking warm places and changes in the skin and coat, such as dry skin, dull coat, increased shedding, thinning hair and skin infections.

Your vet can test for hypothyroidism with a blood test, and supplementation with oral thyroid hormones usually results in a great improvement of symptoms.

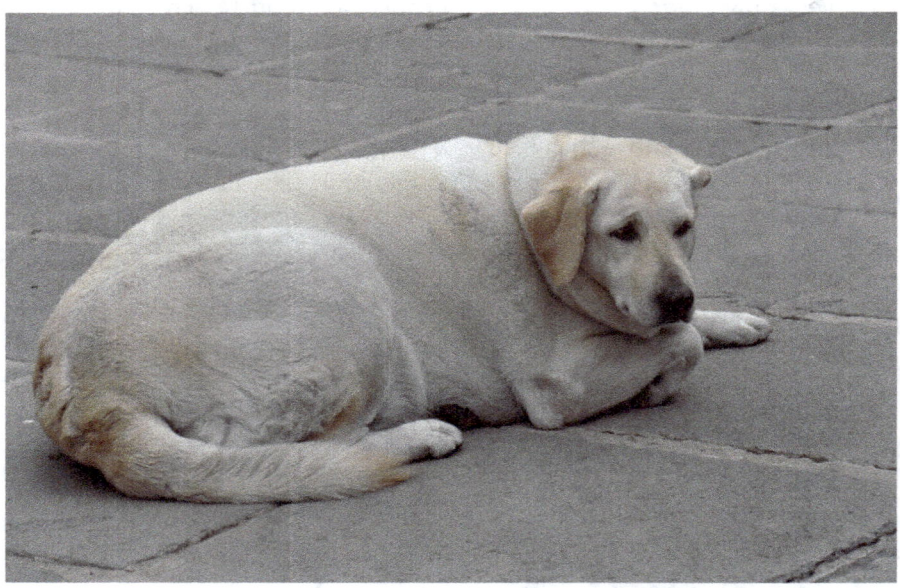

Digestive Conditions

The digestive system is made up of all the organs which are involved in food transit and metabolism, which include the stomach, intestines, pancreas and liver. Digestive system conditions can vary in severity and can cause a variety of symptoms.

Portosystemic Shunt

The liver is vital for converting nutrients into usable forms as well as converting waste products and toxins, ready to be excreted out of the body. However, when a puppy is a fetus, the liver doesn't need to do any work, as no food is being eaten. Therefore, the blood is shunted past the liver via a shortcut, to reduce resistance and ease blood flow.

Towards the end of pregnancy, this shunt closes, and the liver becomes functional, however the Labrador Retriever is at an increased genetic risk of the portosystemic shunt remaining in place, resulting in a decreased use of the liver. This can cause a dangerous build-up of ammonia, from digested proteins, which can have major consequences on the body. Symptoms include increased thirst, vomiting, diarrhea and head pressing against walls (due to a condition called hepatic encephalopathy).

Surgery to close the shunt is the treatment of choice, but for some dogs, the condition must be medically managed with drugs to reduce the fluid build-up on the brain and decrease neurological signs, in combination with a diet which is low in protein to reduce ammonia.

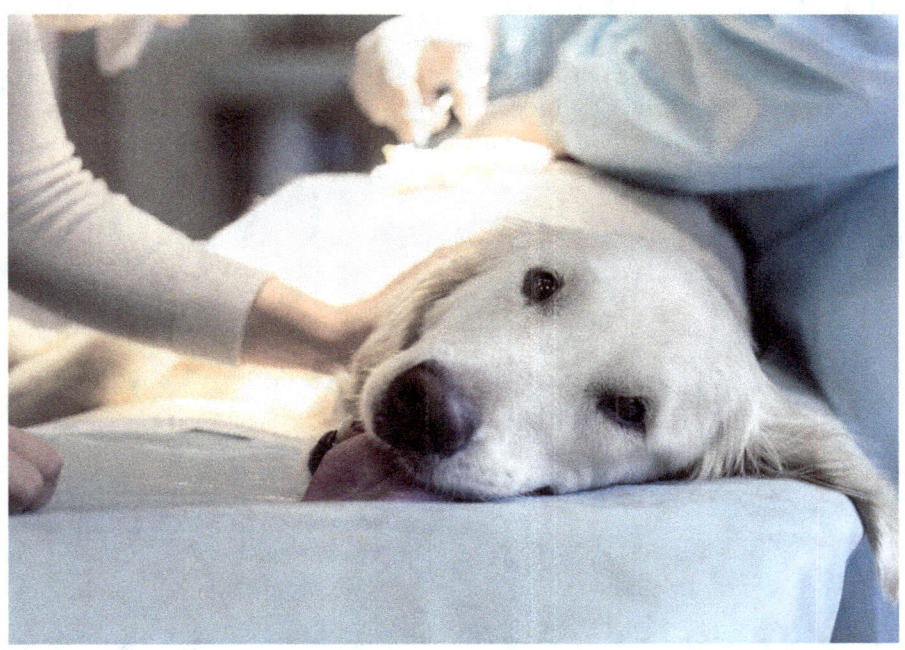

Orthopedic Conditions

"Labs are known for having Hip and Elbow issues, this is why it is important to find a breeder that does the necessary health clearances. Even with proper testing, there still is a chance your puppy will suffer from joint problems, but it's much lower. Maintaining proper diet and limiting exercise until they are fully grown are the best way to prevent your puppy from having joint problems."

Kathy Jackson
Karemy Labs

Orthopedic conditions are any conditions which affect the musculoskeletal makeup of the body. This includes bones, joints, muscles, ligaments and tendons. They are often painful conditions.

Cruciate Ligament Injury

There are two cruciate ligaments which hold the stifle (the equivalent of the dog's knee) together. However, the cranial cruciate ligament, which is the one in the front, can be prone to becoming injured. This causes an instability in the stifle joint and considerable discomfort. Those at a high-

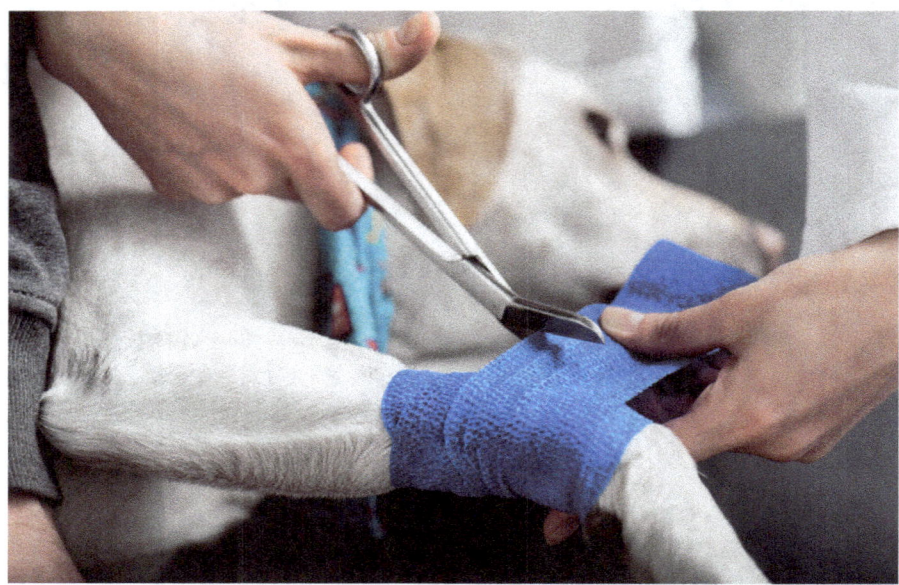

CHAPTER 12 Labrador Retriever Health Conditions

er risk are neutered Labradors, especially males, and those older than four years old.

Cruciate ligament injuries can either be a partial or full tear, and will result in a lameness where your Labrador will probably try to avoid bearing any weight on the leg. They can be treated with several different surgical techniques, or strict crate rest, however in larger dogs such as a Labrador, surgery will provide a better outcome.

Joint Dysplasia, Osteochondrosis and Osteoarthritis

Joint dysplasia of the hip or elbow is a common condition in large breed dogs, and the Labrador is one of the most susceptible. The hip is a ball and socket joint where the head of the femur (ball) fits into a socket in the pelvis. Normally this should be a perfect match, like pieces of a puzzle, but when a dog has hip dysplasia either the ball or the socket is malformed. When the shapes don't match well, it means the joint is less stable when it moves. In severe cases of hip dysplasia, the ball can luxate out of the hip socket as it moves, resulting in a wobbly, swaying gait if viewed from behind.

Elbow dysplasia, on the other hand, has many different elements to it. It is not as simple a joint as the hip, and within the elbow dysplasia condition, there can be multiple abnormalities in development. The most common is-

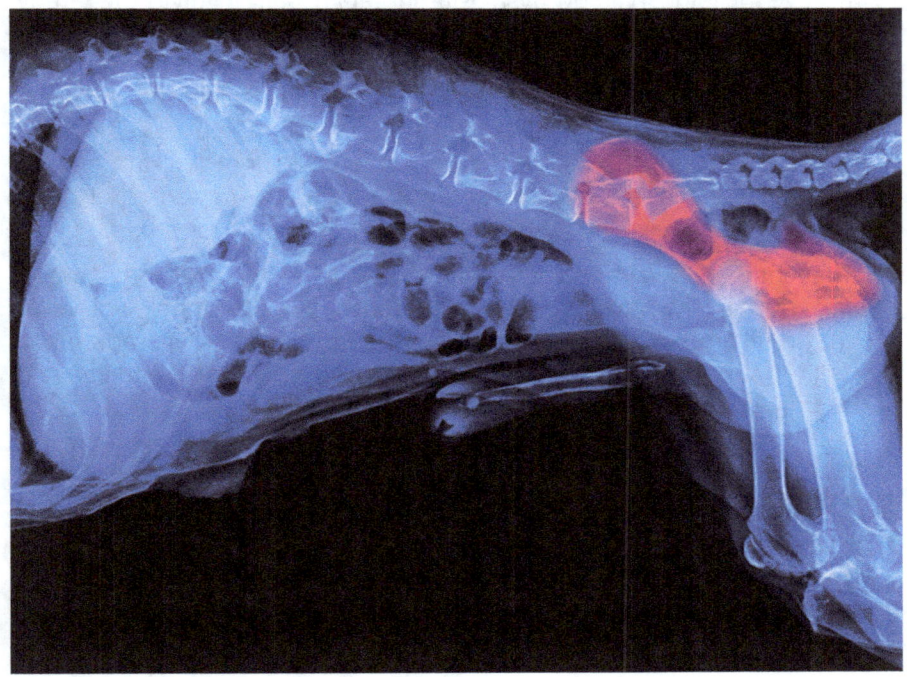

sue in elbow dysplasia is osteochondrosis dissecans (OCD). This is when a flap of joint cartilage separates from the inside joint surface. In addition to this, several different parts of the bones involved in the joint can become detached. These are known as an ununited anconeal process (UAP) and a fragmented medial coronoid process (FMCP). This ultimately leads to lameness or an unusual gait.

Joint dysplasia is usually diagnosed based on X-rays or arthroscopy; however, most veterinarians can have a firm idea that a dog may be suffering from either hip or elbow dysplasia from a simple clinical exam. It is best to understand whether a dog has dysplasia or not from a young age, as if it goes undetected then osteoarthritis will set in at an early stage, which is discussed further in Chapter 16. This can be mitigated with lifestyle changes, such as keeping your dog controlled on walks with minimal jumping, and physical therapies, such as hydrotherapy, to build muscle. Joint supplements also aid in maintaining joint health. The weight of the dog also plays a big role in managing the joints, as a lighter dog will have less gravitational force on the joints, and therefore less stress. Inevitably, all dogs which have joint dysplasia, will one day get osteoarthritis. However, the aim is to avoid this for as long as possible.

For severe cases of both elbow and hip dysplasia, surgery is an option to improve the joint. In elbow dysplasia, surgery usually involves the removal of bone or cartilage fragments. Sometimes a UAP can be reattached with the use of screws if surgery is done at a very young age. With hip dysplasia, the hip joint can be modified by removing the head of the femur, reshaping it and replacing it, or taking it out completely. With both hip and elbow dysplasia, total joint replacement is the gold standard surgical treatment, but with implants can cost a lot, as this surgery requires the immense skill of the surgeon and expensive implant parts.

Prevention is always better than cure, so buying a puppy from a breeder who has had the parents' joints X-rayed and scored will help you avoid purchasing from poor genetics as discussed in Chapter 4. Hip and elbow scoring can be done through the British Kennel Club in the UK and PennHIP at the University of Pennsylvania in the USA.

Limber Tail

Limber tail is also known as 'rudder tail,' 'swimmer's tail,' 'cold water tail,' 'limp tail' and 'broken wag.' It is when the tail becomes limp and has minimal movement in it. This is usually immediately obvious in a Labrador, since their tails are often wagging non-stop.

CHAPTER 12 Labrador Retriever Health Conditions

The condition is usually painful, and you might notice some swelling at the base of the tail, which is where the coccygeal muscle is. It is most common in dogs which are working dogs or dogs who regularly go swimming, and even though the cause and genetic element is not completely clear, an injury to the coccygeal muscle appears to be an element in the condition.

The condition usually self-resolves within a few days to weeks, however your veterinarian will probably prescribe some anti-inflammatories to help your dog with the discomfort.

Panosteitis

Panosteitis is a condition of young (6-16 months old), rapidly growing, large breed dogs, that can be likened to growing pains. It is thought that genetics, stress and autoimmune conditions are all linked to its development; however, the underlying cause is still unknown.

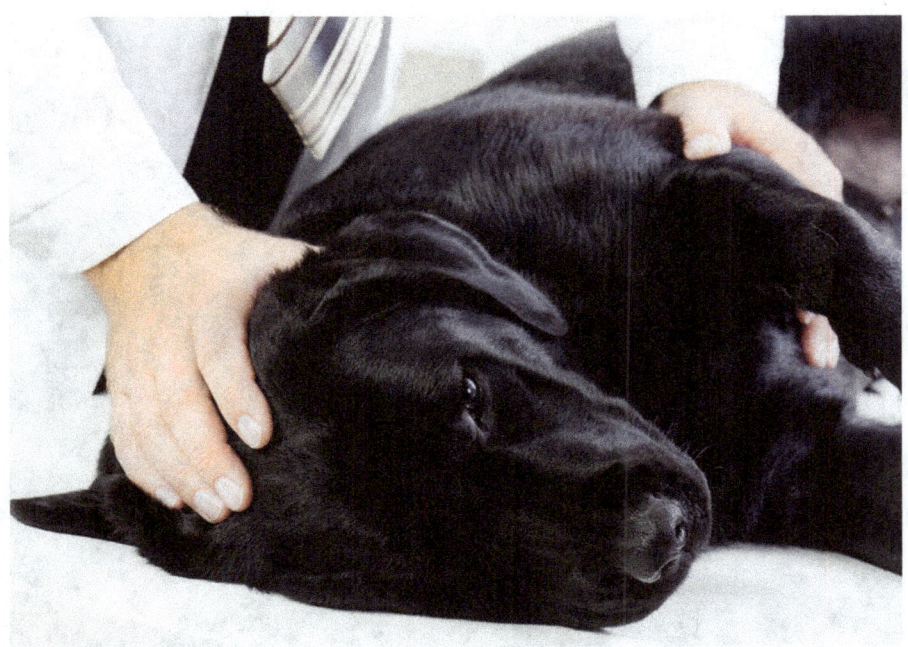

Symptoms include lameness, pain, a temperature, lack of appetite and discomfort when feeling the long bones of the legs. Sometimes just one bone is affected, and other times, multiple bones are involved.

Treatment is aimed at relieving pain; however, the condition is self-limiting and resolves on its own.

Cancers

Cancer is a scary word; however, not all tumors are the same. Some spread around the body rapidly, resulting in a significant shortening of lifespan, whereas others spread very slowly or not at all. Labradors are prone to several types of tumors, some of which are benign, and others which are aggressive.

Hemangiosarcoma

A hemangiosarcoma is a tumor which is vascular in origin, meaning that it is filled with blood and often red in color. They usually appear on older dogs, and in Labradors, the average age for developing a hemangiosarcoma (if developed at all) is 10 years old.

Sometimes it can be difficult to know if your Lab has a hemangiosarcoma, as they are not always evident on the skin. They can develop on the spleen or liver too, or spread from the skin to these organs.

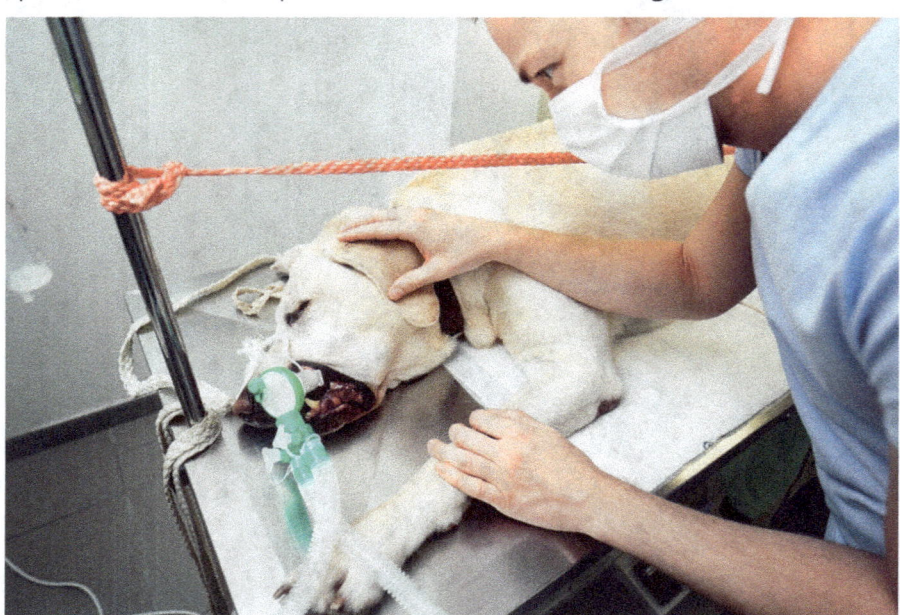

Surgery to remove the tutors is the treatment of choice, and this should be done as early as possible, as since they arise from the blood vessels, they can spread very easily in the blood to other organs.

Lipoma

A lipoma is a benign tumor of the skin, originating from fat cells. They generally occur in obese animals, and Labradors are prone to obesity. They are usually soft and round tumors, which move around if touched.

Even though lipomas are benign and not life-threatening, they can progress to a very large size, resulting in discomfort to your dog.

Surgery is curative, and as long as the tumor is completely excised, the tumor will not come back.

Mast Cell Tumor

Mast cell tumors originate from mast cells, and usually develop in the skin first, before they spread to internal organs. The most common sites are the belly and on the limbs.

Mast cells are white blood cells which release histamine, resulting in these tumors potentially being itchy or uncomfortable, as well as increasing and decreasing in size. They are graded on a scale of I-III, with I being low grade, and III being aggressive and high grade. The grade of the tumor determines how likely it is to spread around the body and cause problems.

Surgical removal is the treatment of choice. However, for grade II or III tumors, or tumors with evidence of spread around the body, this might be followed up by chemotherapy.

Osteosarcoma

An osteosarcoma is a bone tumor, which can be aggressive. The most common bones affected are the radius, the humerus, the femur or the tibia. The most common clinical sign is lameness, in combination with swelling of the bone.

Since the bones affected are usually the bones of the leg, leg amputation may be necessary, followed by chemotherapy, however, the prognosis is still poor, with untreated dogs living no more than a few months, and dogs who have had surgery, only living on average an extra five months.

Neurological Conditions

Neurological conditions which manifest at a young age are often hereditary. These are conditions which affect the brain and the spinal cord. Conditions which appear later in life are less likely to be linked to genetics.

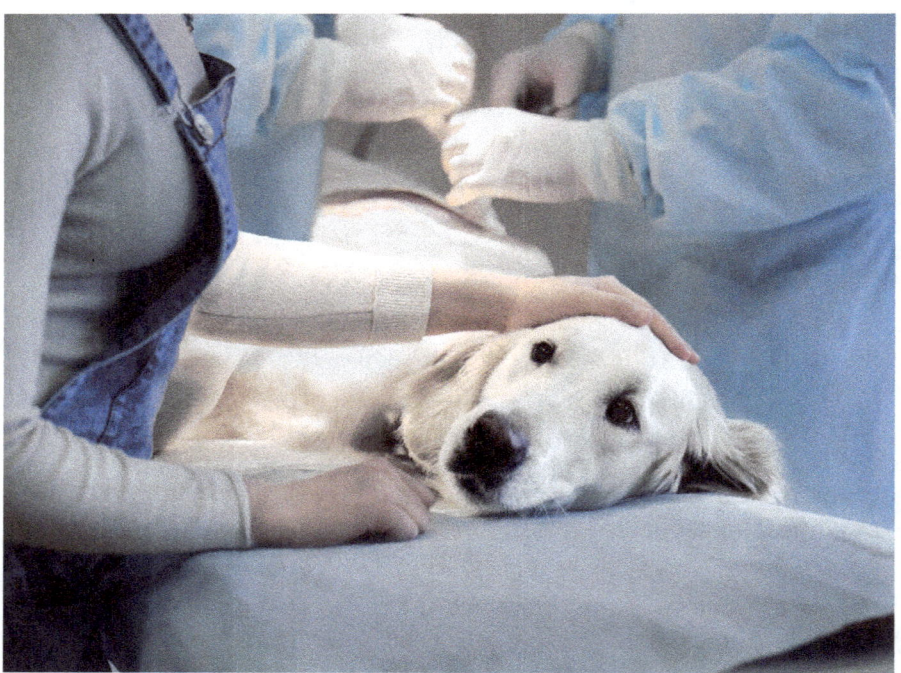

Epilepsy

Epilepsy is a condition that causes seizures, however not all seizures are caused by epilepsy. Other causes of seizures, such as brain abnormalities, encephalitis and hepatic encephalopathy, need to be ruled out first, before a diagnosis of epilepsy can be made.

Even though seizures can be traumatic for both you and your Labrador, there are medications available to reduce the frequency of the seizures and allow your Lab to live a relatively normal life. Nevertheless, if the seizure lasts over five minutes, or seizures come in clusters (several in a short space of time), this is an indication that you should urgently get your Labrador to the vet for a reevaluation.

CHAPTER 12 Labrador Retriever Health Conditions

Ocular Conditions

Ocular conditions relate to conditions of any of the structures in the eye.

Cataracts

A cataract is a condition of the lens in the eye, where it becomes white and opaque, leading to blindness. The lens is the part of the eye which changes shape to be able to direct the light onto the back of the eye appropriately. If this doesn't work, vision becomes blurry. Cataracts are when the lens starts to become opaque. Some dogs develop them in just one eye, and other dogs develop them bilaterally.

A veterinarian will diagnose cataracts by looking in the eye with an ophthalmoscope. This is a device which shines light in the eye and bounces it back to a magnifying glass. If the light shines all the way to the back of the eye, where the retina is, then the lens is normal. However, if the light reflects off the lens instead, then it has developed a cataract.

Nuclear sclerosis, to the naked eye, looks very similar to a cataract. This is a normal condensing together of the lens fibers, which happens with age. However, it is not opaque, and therefore with the ophthalmoscope, a vet can look to the very back of the eye.

There is nothing medical that can be applied to the eye for a cataract. A veterinary ophthalmologist however can replace the lens in a referral hospital setting, but this is an uncommon operation and requires extensive technical expertise.

Progressive Retinal Atrophy

Abbreviated to PRA, progressive retinal atrophy is a recessive inherited disease. It can be tested for in breeding animals, and it is the responsible thing to do for anyone intending on breeding a Labrador.

It causes gradual vision loss, which begins with night blindness. This is due to the back of the eye, known as the retina, gradually deteriorating.

There is no treatment for PRA, and it will always lead to blindness of both eyes. Ultimately, this is not a death sentence, as dogs can live happily with no sight, especially highly intelligent dogs such as the Labrador.

Urinary Conditions

Urinary conditions are conditions which affect the kidneys, bladder, or the tubes connecting them, known as the ureters and urethra.

Ectopic Ureters

HELPFUL TIP
Why You Should Consider Pet Insurance

As you're looking for a vet who will care for your dog throughout its life, you should consider purchasing pet insurance. If your Lab gets hit by a car or gets cancer, will you be able to afford treatment? Pet insurance isn't right for everybody, but it can help manage the cost of vet care for your Lab.

The ureter is the tube which carries urine from the kidneys to the bladder, where it is stored until there is enough for the dog to void it. The word ectopic means outside, and ectopic ureters are exactly that—the ureters come to an end outside the bladder, usually into the urethra, which is the tube which carries the urine from the bladder to outside the body. As a result, dogs which have ectopic ureters will constantly leak urine. Generally, the condition is more common in females, and is usually apparent before one year of age.

There is nothing medical which can be done for the condition, and surgery is the only option to correct the anatomical abnormality. While waiting for the surgery, the hair should be kept short around the area where the urine is leaking to avoid urine scald, and the area must be cleaned regularly.

Respiratory Conditions

Respiratory conditions are conditions which affect your Labrador's breathing. They can affect the nose, nostrils, throat (larynx and pharynx), trachea, bronchi and lungs.

CHAPTER 12   Labrador Retriever Health Conditions

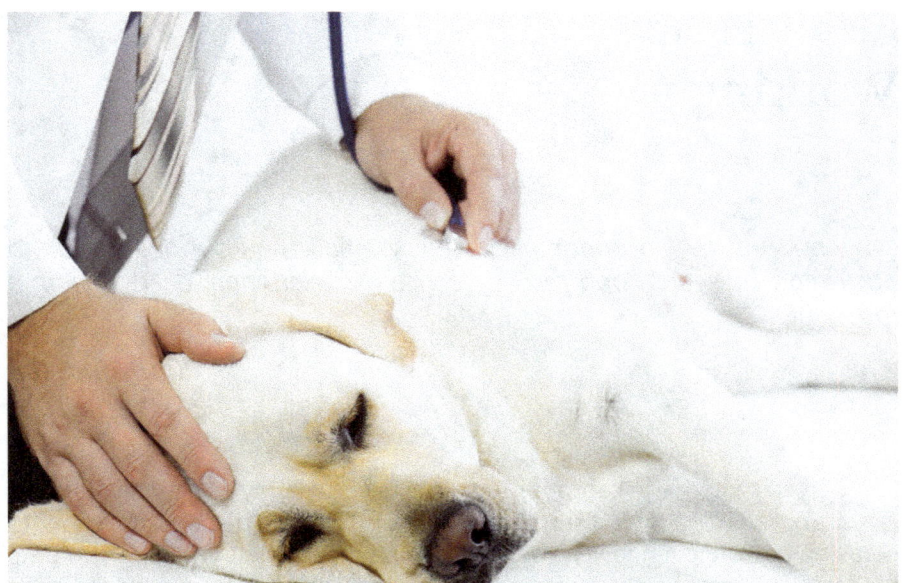

Laryngeal Paralysis

The larynx is the cartilage at the top of the throat which controls the opening to the lungs. When a dog is suffering from laryngeal paralysis, one or both sides of the larynx do not open fully when breathing in, narrowing the airway. Symptoms include a cough, voice changes and loud breathing, and in severe cases, it can cause difficulty in breathing and collapse.

Treatment involves relieving signs of a narrowed airway, which can be done with anti-inflammatories in some cases. Severe cases might require a tracheotomy. Surgery can be done to open the airway more, and it has a good success rate.

***

Labrador Retrievers are prone to more health conditions than the average purebred dog, however that's not to say that all Labradors will develop a condition in their lifetime. Nevertheless, it is important to understand what conditions Labradors are prone to, so that you can be aware of them and pick up any presenting symptoms early. That way your Lab will have the best prognosis going forward.

CHAPTER 13
Working

"Above all, the Labrador is versatile. We have had our dogs go on to do avalanche search and rescue, service work, hunting, or just being a family pet."

Kathy Jackson
Karemy Labs

Even though the Labrador Retriever is very happy as a family dog, the breed has a long history in the working world. The Labrador's innate pleasing nature, trainability and intelligence means that whatever he puts his mind to, he can be trained to do. Even if it seems that your docile companion would prefer to take a seat next to your side, lurking inside him are instincts that would make him an excellent companion out in the working world too. Nevertheless, whether or not you intend to have a working Labrador, this chapter will help you to learn how adaptable and capable the Labrador Retriever truly is.

Photo Courtesy of Mike Valant

CHAPTER 13   Working

Photo Courtesy of Anne Lowry

Field Work

Labrador Retrievers are known as "gun dogs," as their original role when the breed was brought from Newfoundland to the United Kingdom in the nineteenth century was to be a companion to men or women who wished to shoot wild game. The retriever sub-group, in the gun dog category, includes the Labrador Retriever, Golden Retriever, Flat-coated Retriever and Chesapeake Bay Retriever. While all very similar, Labradors clearly lead the way in popularity. This is because they have excellent game finding ability, they are extremely trainable, and their mouths are very soft, meaning the game does not get damaged when they pick it up. In addition to this, Labradors are tough, with a waterproof coat, and athletic enough to withstand long days out in the field.

The main role of a Labrador when out in the field is to bring back shot game to his master. This is an important job, as not only is it difficult for a hunter to retrieve what he has shot without disturbing the surrounding area and future game for shooting, but it also ensures that any wounded animal is rapidly retrieved and humanely dispatched.

There are some slight differences in the way field work is conducted between the US and the UK. In the US, Labradors are expected to retrieve either upland game or waterfowl. Both are popular types of shoots, and Labradors are regularly expected to swim to retrieve game. Some Amer-

Photo Courtesy of
Robert Cassidy
Cassidy Photography

CHAPTER 13 Working

ican Labradors also have been taught to point, to help their owners find the game, however this is now mainly left up to Setter and Pointer breeds.

In the UK, retrieving dogs are known as "peg dogs" and wait to be given the signal by the "guns" (those doing the shooting) to retrieve game birds. Labradors can also be used by a team of "pickers up," who follow the "beaters" that use Spaniels to help flush the birds. Most of this shooting is inland, where pheasants, grouse, partridges and woodcocks are usually shot.

> **QUOTE**
> **Training Yourself**
>
> *In order to really enjoy a dog, one doesn't merely try to train him to be semi-human. The point of it is to open oneself to the possibility of becoming partly a dog.*
> **— Edward Hoagland**

Wildfowling is a less common type of hunting in the UK, unlike the US where waterfowl hunting is very popular. But Britain has an extensive coastline, and plenty of opportunities to hunt geese and duck on the foreshore. Labradors excel at retrieving these types of birds, and swimming in cold water is no deterrent for them.

If you are thinking that it would be nice to try your hand at shooting with your Labrador, it is not difficult to start training your Labrador to have a working role. Obedience is key, and the basic commands of 'sit', 'heel' and 'come' are vital. When working out in the field, most signals are given by hand or a whistle. The best way to learn these is constant practice with dummies, and plenty of shadowing more experienced gun dog trainers. Formal gun dog training should not start until at least six or seven months old, and training can be delegated to a professional gun dog trainer if you're inexperienced.

If you are keen to work your Labrador in the field, but are a non-shooting owner, Field Trials might be worth exploring. In the US, a 'hunt test' is a non-competitive assessment for gun dogs. There are a series of predetermined retrieves which every dog must attempt under the same conditions. In the UK however, 'gun dog working tests' (GWTs) are competitive and can use different types of retrieves for each competing dog. They also use both dead birds and dummies. The judge looks for the dog's game-finding ability, good manners and soft mouth.

The best way to get into working and training your Labrador would be to contact the North American Hunting Retriever Association in the USA, to find your local club. In the UK, the hunting community is a little harder to break into, but joining the Gundog Club or offering to help out on some shoots in the summertime, will help you make great contacts.

Assistance Dogs for the Disabled

The gentle nature and high intelligence of a Labrador makes them perfect for being trained as assistance dogs for the disabled.

Labradors are by far the most popular breed of Guide Dogs. Their job allows their owners to live a more independent life as well as be involved more in their community.

Guide dog training can cost tens of thousands of dollars, and it is mainly done through non-profit organizations, so it's no light commitment for a Labrador to start on the road to training for this important role. Most guide dogs are bred from specialist breeding programs, targeted at producing puppies with all the required traits and a clean bill of health. From eight weeks old, the dogs begin informal training. Up until 12-18 months, they are introduced to a variety of different environments, and continually assessed to see whether their character is suited for the job of a guide dog. If they pass this stage, they enter formal training. However, even though formal training is intense, they still live in a home environment and are allowed time to play, walk and nap like any other dog. When they are two years old, they are then paired with their new owner, who will have also gone through some training.

Even though guide dog training is what most people think of when training a Labrador for a disabled person, Labradors can also make excellent assistance dogs for a variety of conditions. Labradors can pick up everyday items which might be difficult to reach or pick up, such as phones, wallets and keys. They can also help with dressing, collecting mail, loading the washing machine, opening doors, pressing the button on a pedestrian crossing, alerting their owners to a noise and vitally, providing a wonderful source of companionship. Therefore, an assistance Labrador can help their owner feel less isolated and have a greater sense of independence.

Labradors are often also used as support dogs for children with autism or people with emotional difficulties. They are also able to support owners with medical conditions, and alert owners to impending seizures, a drop in blood sugar levels for diabetics and many other medical emergencies. They are also commonly used as therapy dogs, that visit hospitals, nursing homes and care residences for short term interaction.

It's no wonder that Labradors are so popular in the role of assistance dogs, as they are incredibly versatile in their abilities.

CHAPTER 13 Working

*Photo Courtesy Of
Autumn Paige Steed*

Photo Courtesy of Lisa Higbee

Search and Rescue

In the wake of natural disasters, such as earthquakes, avalanches and tornadoes, Labradors can be used as search and rescue dogs to help detect signs of life buried beneath rubble. Their excellent noses, pinpoint hearing, trainability, and light footsteps help them to navigate through disaster sites with more agility and surefootedness than humans could. In these situations, time is of the essence, and can mean the difference between life and death, so the fact that a Labrador can do the work of a team of people makes them the unsung heroes of the rescue effort.

Labradors can also be used in the search for missing people. These include people who have run away from home, lost hikers, or elderly or confused people who don't know where they are.

Official search and rescue training starts at around 18 months old, and takes between six months and two years. The handler also goes through this training, and it is important that there is a true bond between the Labrador and the handler to be effective.

HELPFUL TIP: Training Your Lab

Labrador Retrievers are highly trainable, which is why they are so commonly used as guide dogs, service dogs, and therapy dogs. They are motivated by food, toys, or even just praise. Use this to your advantage to ensure your Lab is a well-trained good citizen.

CHAPTER 13   Working

Police and Armed Forces Dogs

In the armed forces, Labradors can use their exceptional sense of smell to detect pieces of explosive material. They are highly regarded for saving many lives of both soldiers and civilians from unexploded IEDs and active minefields.

They can also serve in other law enforcement roles. Police and custom officers regularly employ Labradors to detect drugs and other illegal items, such as weapons, explosives, and even people being brought into the country. Labradors are regularly seen with police officers at airports and ferry terminals. Even though they don't possess the natural aggression of police dogs who perform protection duties, such as German Shepherds, their excellent nose is why many Labradors are employed as specialty detector dogs.

When a detector dog picks up a target scent, he will show his handler a signal. This is usually either scratching next to it, or sitting down. A handler of a detector dog needs to be completely in tune with the language of his dog, to pick up on all his signals.

A detector dog can make quick and easy work of examining large areas. A normal border control officer will be able to search a vehicle in 20 minutes, whereas a detector dog will only take five minutes. This ensures traffic can keep flowing and the border does not experience long delays.

***

Photo Courtesy of Danielle Zentic

Due to the good nature and trainability of the Labrador, they can put their paw to almost any job required of them. Most working dogs are destined to their roles; however, it doesn't mean a rescue Labrador or your pet Labrador is not able to do the job. The breed's intelligence is second to none, and this is something that you can use to best advantage when training your Labrador at home.

CHAPTER 14
Breeding

Deciding about Breeding

Labradors are one of the most popular breeds in the world, and as a result, also one of the most frequently bred. It may be tempting, if you have a Labrador, to want to breed your dog. After all, not only are Labrador puppies cute, but they are in high demand and therefore you can easily find homes for them.

Nevertheless, these are not reasons to breed your Labrador. Labradors have a huge number of genetic diseases. This is due to indiscriminate breeding and poor choices of breeding mates, as well as lack of knowledge about genetically linked health problems. Just because your Labrador has a wonderful nature, doesn't make it an ideal Labrador to breed.

Labrador puppies can reach a high price; however, you shouldn't be quick to assume that you can make a lot of money from a litter. You would need to invest in genetic testing, hip and elbow scoring, and provide excellent nutrition for your Labrador throughout mating and pregnancy. This can cost thousands of dollars, and there's always the risk of an emergency caesarian section if your dog struggles giving birth, which would cost several thousand dollars more. Breeding puppies is certainly not going to make a quick buck.

Breeding requires extensive knowledge, time and money, so if you are looking at becoming a dedicated Labrador Retriever breeder, then this chapter will give you some basic knowledge to get you on your way. It can be extremely rewarding to contribute to improving the genetics of the Labrador breed with a healthy, impressive litter of offspring, but first make sure that you are breeding your dog for the right reasons.

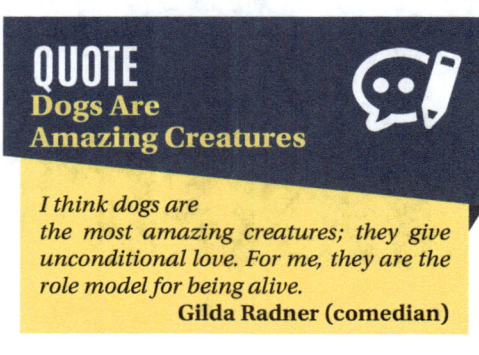

QUOTE
Dogs Are Amazing Creatures

I think dogs are the most amazing creatures; they give unconditional love. For me, they are the role model for being alive.
Gilda Radner (comedian)

CHAPTER 14   Breeding

Mating

If you have decided that you wish to pursue mating your Labrador, whether you have a male or female, you should first make sure your Labrador is healthy and of high genetic quality. Your veterinarian should take X-rays for hip and elbow scoring, and blood tests for genetic testing. Tests can include centronuclear myopathy, exercise induced collapse, hereditary nasal parakeratosis, progressive retinal atrophy and skeletal dwarfism. A positive test doesn't mean your Labrador will become ill one day, but it means that there is potential for your Labrador's puppies to develop a disease. The results will come back as either clear, carrier (where there is one normal gene and one mutant gene, and therefore half the offspring will be affected), or affected (where there are two mutant genes). It is also recommended that your Labrador have a specialist ophthalmological examination.

If you have performed all the required tests and the results are clear, then you can look for a mate for your dog. A mate should also have had clear tests. They also should not have a bloodline where there is excessive inbreeding, which can be seen by repeating names within the family tree.

If you have a female Labrador, she can only mate when she is in season. This is also known as being 'in heat' or 'in estrus,' and the terms are used interchangeably. On average, this is roughly every six months, and lasts for

approximately a week. The rest of the time, your dog is reproductively inactive and will not be able to conceive. Signs that your Labrador is in season include swelling and redness of the vulva, a slight bloody discharge, and attractiveness to male dogs. If you need to travel far to the stud dog, it may already be too late in your dog's cycle (by the time you notice) to travel to the stud dog. This can be overcome with blood tests. Your veterinarian can run blood tests to confirm where in her cycle she is, and predict the best days for her to breed to increase the chances of conception. If she is ready, the stud dog will mount her and then turn around to face away from her. This is known as a tie. Once tied, if the dogs are forcefully separated, it can cause considerable damage to the stud dog.

Your dog must be allowed to have her first season before being mated. She can be mated between her second season up until five years old. After this, it is not recommended that you breed your dog further as producing a litter of puppies requires the body to take on a great deal of strain, which an older dog might not be able to handle.

Pregnancy

After mating, you will understandably be impatient to know whether your dog is pregnant. Pregnancy lasts for just over two months, approximately 63 days, but it is difficult to know very early on whether she has

conceived. A blood test can be performed at 22 days, but a less invasive ultrasound scan is better, which can be done from 42 days. It is difficult to know how large the litter will be without an X-ray to count the fetal skeletons; however, this should not be routinely performed, as it can damage fetal development.

Pregnancy is stressful on the body and therefore you should provide your Labrador with the best quality diet to stay healthy. This should be a high energy diet, and towards the latter part of the pregnancy, can be a puppy diet. This will provide her with more calcium for the developing bones of the puppies, as well as calcium to start producing milk. Your dog can be walked daily, but not excessively. Twenty minutes is ideal, and you should discourage jumping and uncontrolled running. She should be allowed plenty of time to rest too.

When your dog is in her last week of pregnancy, her teats will become swollen, ready to produce milk and she might start acting motherly to her toys. She is likely to start creating a nest space to give birth in. You should not disrupt your Labrador too much when she is doing this, as it is her readying process, and disruptions may place undue stress on her body and emotions.

Birthing

Labor and birth can be a worrying time for everyone; however, it is best to try to give your Labrador as much space and peace as possible. Most mothers have a natural instinct about what to do when giving birth, and will not need your assistance. Nevertheless, keeping watch from a distance to make sure everything is going smoothly is advisable.

Birth is imminent when your Labrador's temperature drops below 100 degrees Fahrenheit. A normal temperature is between 101 and 102.5 degrees. Towards the end of pregnancy, most breeders will take their Labrador's temperature twice a day to pick up on the temperature drop. Your dog is likely to show signs of labor which include pacing, whining, and pushing. Do not panic if this goes on for a while. There can even be up to two hours in between puppies being delivered.

Each puppy will come out individually, usually with the amniotic sac still around them. The mother will pull the sac open after the puppy is born and lick away the fluid. This stimulates the puppy to breathe, as well as warms it up and dries it off. Sometimes breeders like to step in at this stage and pick up the puppy to rub them vigorously with a towel. This is not always neces-

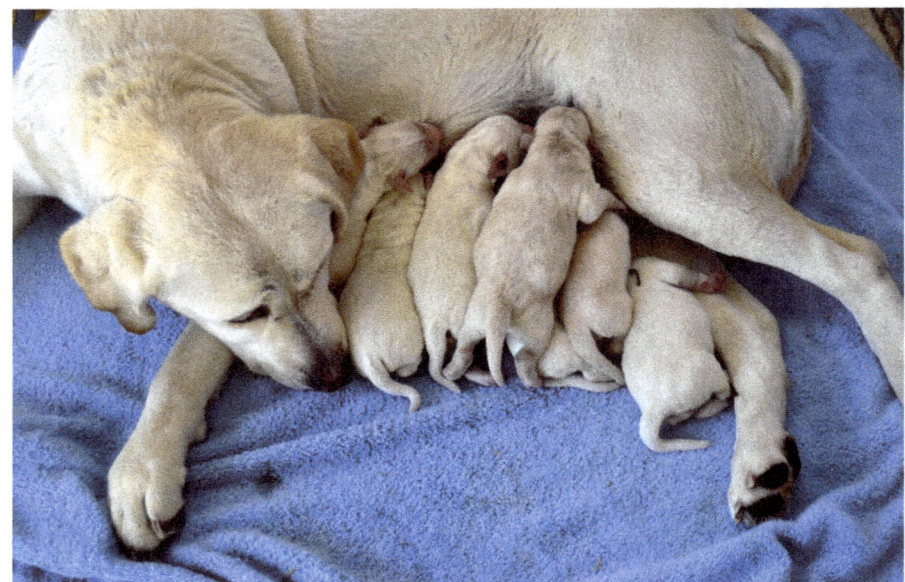

sary, but if your Labrador is a first-time mom, or not showing very good instincts, then your action could potentially save many of the puppies.

If these symptoms go on for more than two hours with no puppy being born, there is green or black discharge, or there has been a temperature drop over 24 hours ago, these are signs that you should take your dog to your veterinarian. He might start by giving her a shot of oxytocin to stimulate uterine muscle contraction, or he may take her straight to surgery for a caesarian section. The sooner you take your Labrador to the vet in such situations, the higher the chance that all the puppies will be alive.

The afterbirth will probably be eaten by your dog, which gives her a boost of nutrients. This is really important, as giving birth is a tiring process, and her body will now be under a lot of strain to produce milk.

Aftercare

After all the puppies have been delivered, you should gently check them each for abnormalities. Open their mouths and make sure there is no cleft palate and that there is not an excess of mucus. Also check they are breathing properly and don't have any major birth defects, such as a large umbilical hernia. If any are still slightly damp, you can dry them off further with a towel.

CHAPTER 14   Breeding

The mother can then be given a warm sponge bath to clean up, and then she and the litter should be allowed to rest somewhere warm and free of draughts. It should be comfortable, but soft bedding should be avoided as the puppies can become smothered on these surfaces.

Some light discharge from the vulva is normal after giving birth, and this might go on for a week or so. It should be pink, red or brown, but if it is profuse, black, green or smelly, you should take your dog to the vet. It could be a sign that there is still afterbirth left in, or even a dead fetus.

Once your Labrador has settled into her role of being a mother, and the puppies are suckling well, you should take them to your local veterinary practice for a check over. A good point for this is at about one week old, unless you notice any abnormalities with either your dog or the puppies.

Raising Puppies

Finally, raising puppies is the fun bit, especially when they open their eyes and are starting to run around. You have a great responsibility to find them potential homes and you should not be shy to say no to a home which you don't feel is suitable. You need to vet the new owners as much as they need to come and check out the puppies.

You can start trying to find new homes from when the puppies are a few weeks old. You can advertise them on the Kennel Club website to ensure that prospective owners are dedicated to buying a puppy from a reputable breeder, rather than the cheapest one they find.

The puppies should not be released until they are at least eight weeks old. If a buyer wishes to reserve one, you can place a colorful collar on it to distinguish it from the rest.

When the puppies are around four weeks old, they might start showing interest in their mother's food. Even though milk still makes up a large portion of their diet, it is okay to start letting the pups explore dog food. This is best done by offering them puppy food, which can either be wet, or soaked kibble. Between four and eight weeks, they will slowly decrease their milk intake and switch over to exclusively dog food.

All responsible dog breeders will make sure their puppies are dewormed, microchipped and have had their first puppy vaccine before they go to their new homes. Puppies need to be wormed against roundworms at 2, 4, 6, 8 and 12 weeks of age as they are particularly susceptible at a young age to pick up worms. They only need to have flea treatment if they have fleas, and if they need to be treated, it should be done so with a product which is suitable for puppies, as many flea products cannot be used on very young or very small animals.

CHAPTER 14 Breeding

***

It can be really rewarding to know you are contributing to producing Labradors of a high genetic standard, to try to improve the gene pool of the breed. However, you should not assume that breeding your dog and managing puppies will be easy, as it will take time, patience, financial investment and a great deal of knowledge to do it properly. Also, once you breed more than a certain number of litters on one premises in a year (usually three, although may vary by state), you are classified as a commercial breeder, and will have to be licensed and inspected. So if you are not planning to become a professional breeder, it is best to leave it up to the established breeding kennels.

CHAPTER 15
Showing

Selecting a Dog for Showing

The Labrador is a beautiful-looking dog, and many proud owners are eager to show off their dog's good looks by entering dog shows. Of course, the Labrador is also a working dog, and just as much a superstar of working trials as conformation classes. So, your Labrador has plenty of potential to bring home the trophies, and if that is something that appeals to you, your first consideration should be selecting the right dog.

There are many local, fun dog shows, where anything goes. Your dog will not need a pedigree certificate, or have to conform rigidly to the breed standard. He can be neutered, unneutered, docked or undocked. He may be any shade on the Labrador color spectrum, with atypical markings or pigmentation, and he will still have a chance of a ribbon, as long as the judge sees the beauty and character that you love in him. Local shows are ideal if you have a rescue Labrador with bags of personality but no pedigree papers. If you don't aspire to anything higher than local shows, then your choice of Labrador may simply be guided by your heart. If, however, you wish to enter Kennel Club shows, you will need to be governed by the rules right from the day you first pick out a breeder.

HELPFUL TIP
Socialization and Service Dogs

Have you ever seen service dog puppy handlers? You'll see them in all sort of places. Service dogs need to get used to all sorts of other dogs, people, situations, sights, sounds, smells, and more. Think that socialization is only for service dogs? Think again. Socialization is a key part of raising any healthy, happy, and well-behaved Labrador Retriever.

For higher level shows, you will need to select a Kennel Club registered dog from Kennel Club registered parents. If you are looking for a dog to show in working classes, you will need to look at kennels producing sporting dogs. Whereas if your interest is in the show ring, you will need to look at kennels where the breeding stock can boast show champions. This will mean your puppy has the best chance of inheriting the genetics that the judges are looking for.

CHAPTER 15 Showing

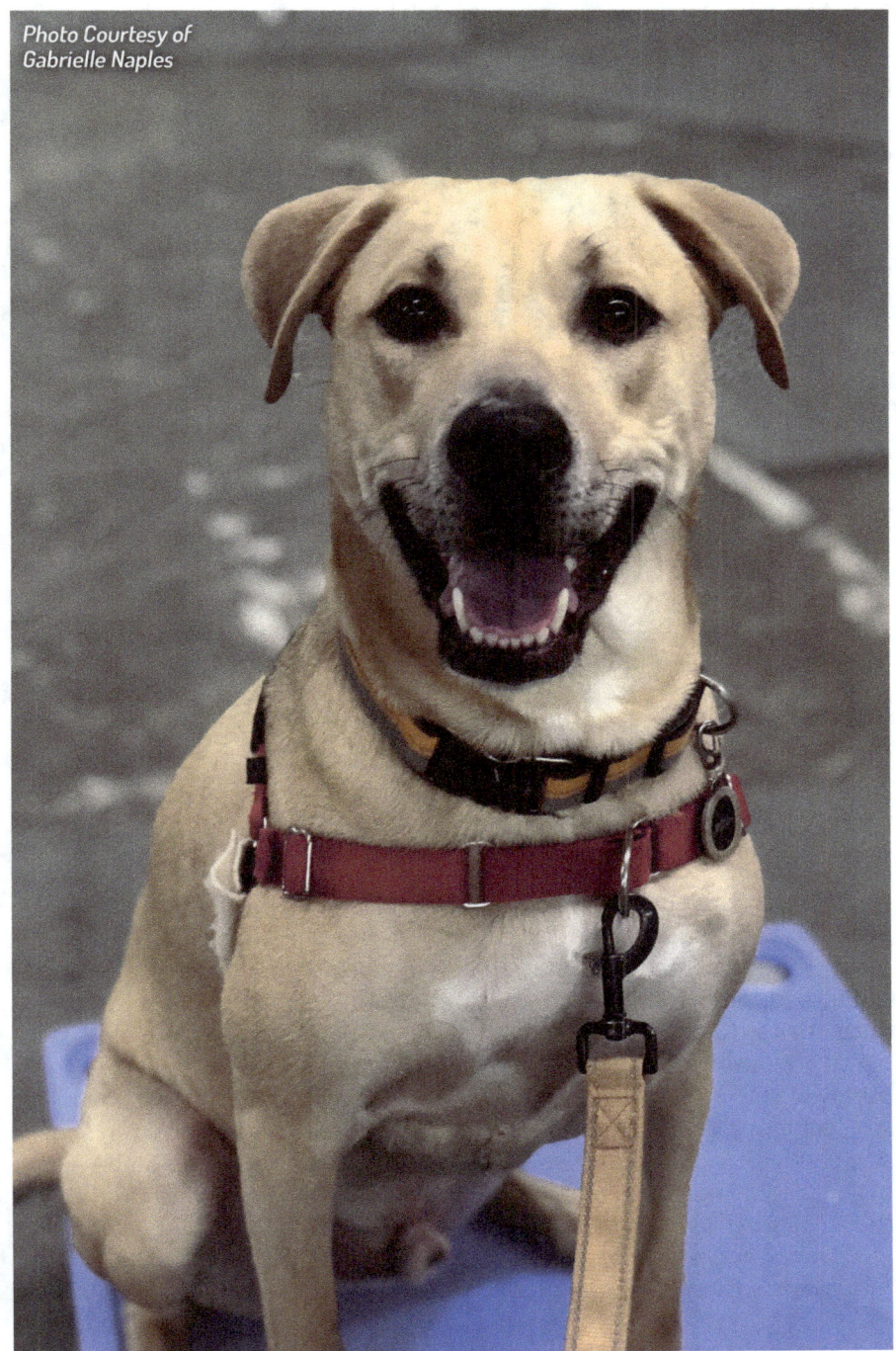

Photo Courtesy of Gabrielle Naples

Before going to look at a litter, you should thoroughly acquaint yourself with the Kennel Club breed standard for the Labrador Retriever in your country. You should be aware that the breed standard is updated from time to time, and can vary between countries.

In order for your Labrador to win Kennel Club conformation classes, he needs to conform as closely as possible to the blueprint of the breed, set out in the breed standard. The breed standard describes the perfect Labrador, and the model to which all Labrador breeders should aspire to produce. It aims to promote the health of the breed, however some of its standards are more cosmetic. You should be aware however that in choosing a puppy whose appearance can never match the breed standard, due to his size, color or pigmentation, means you will be restricted to local fun shows, and cannot compete with the Kennel Club. Above all, you should be aware of the disqualifications for showing a Labrador Retriever, which in the USA are: *"1. Any deviation from the height prescribed in the Standard. 2. A thoroughly pink nose or one lacking in any pigment. 3. Eye rims without pigment. 4. Docking or otherwise altering the length or natural carriage of the tail. 5. Any other*

CHAPTER 15 Showing

color or a combination of colors other than black, yellow or chocolate as described in the Standard." (AKC breed standard, 1994)

The other important thing to note is that the fundamental purpose of conformation shows is for the evaluation of breeding stock. Therefore, your dog cannot be neutered. Neutered dogs can compete, but only in certain activity classes. In some countries, such as the UK, they may be shown with a special exemption certificate, but in practice are unlikely to be placed as highly as entire dogs. Labrador Retrievers should also never be docked, as their greatest attribute is their "otter tail," which is highly rewarded in the show ring.

When you view the litter of puppies, which may be as early as five weeks, it will be very hard to spot show potential unless you have considerable experience. You will therefore have to rely on the size, appearance and temperament of both parents, as well as any show successes they may have notched up. The breeder is the best judge of how the puppies will turn out, and he will be able to guide your choice. You should be aware though that he may have set aside the most promising show champions for himself. That is the breeder's prerogative, and in the interest of future generations of Labradors born to his kennels. That is not to say every puppy in the litter doesn't have show potential: with good genetics, they may all be future champions.

Breed Standards

Every country has its own idea of the perfect physical attributes of the Labrador Retriever, so you should make sure you check the breed standard for the country in which you wish to show your dog.

The main distinction in the public mind, is between the American and English Labrador types, with the American Labrador being taller, slimmer, finer and more athletic, with longer legs, a narrower head, longer neck and longer muzzle, and a thinner coat and tail than the English Labrador. However, the American Labrador represents the working dog, and the English

Photo Courtesy of Anne Lowry

CHAPTER 15 Showing

Labrador is regarded as a show dog, so even in the USA, the breed standard for conformation classes leans towards the English type. The American Kennel Club Official Standard is given below. If you are in a different country, your breed standard may be found on your country's Kennel Club website, where you can be sure it is the most up to date version.

American Kennel Club (USA) Official Standard for the Labrador Retriever (1994):

General Appearance: The Labrador Retriever is a strongly built, medium-sized, short-coupled, dog possessing a sound, athletic, well-balanced conformation that enables it to function as a retrieving gun dog; the substance and soundness to hunt waterfowl or upland game for long hours under difficult conditions; the character and quality to win in the show ring; and the temperament to be a family companion. Physical features and mental characteristics should denote a dog bred to perform as an efficient Retriever of game with a stable temperament suitable for a variety of pursuits beyond the hunting environment.

The most distinguishing characteristics of the Labrador Retriever are its short, dense, weather resistant coat; an "otter" tail; a clean-cut head with broad back skull and moderate stop; powerful jaws; and its "kind", friendly eyes, expressing character, intelligence and good temperament. Above all, a Labrador Retriever must be well balanced, enabling it to move in the show ring or work in the field with little or no effort. The typical Labrador possesses style and quality without over refinement, and substance without lumber or cloddiness. The Labrador is bred primarily as a working gun dog; structure and soundness are of great importance.

Size, Proportion and Substance: *Size-* The height at the withers for a dog is 22½ to 24½ inches; for a bitch is 21½ to 23½ inches. Any variance greater than ½ inch above or below these heights is a disqualification. Approximate weight of dogs and bitches in working condition: dogs 65 to 80 pounds; bitches 55 to 70 pounds. The minimum height ranges set forth in the paragraph above shall not apply to dogs or bitches under twelve months of age.

Proportion- Short-coupled; length from the point of the shoulder to the point of the rump is equal to or slightly longer than the distance from the withers to the ground. Distance from the elbow to the ground should be equal to one half of the height at the withers. The brisket should extend to the elbows, but not perceptibly deeper. The body must be of sufficient length to permit a straight, free and efficient stride; but the dog should never appear low and long or tall and leggy in outline.

Substance- Substance and bone proportionate to the overall dog. Light, "weedy" individuals are definitely incorrect; equally objectionable are cloddy lumbering specimens. Labrador Retrievers shall be shown in working condition well-muscled and without excess fat.

Head: *Skull*- The skull should be wide; well-developed but without exaggeration. The skull and foreface should be on parallel planes and of approximately equal length. There should be a moderate stop-the brow slightly pronounced so that the skull is not absolutely in a straight line with the nose. The brow ridges aid in defining the stop. The head should be clean-cut and free from fleshy cheeks; the bony structure of the skull chiseled beneath the eye with no prominence in the cheek. The skull may show some median line; the occipital bone is not conspicuous in mature dogs. Lips should not be squared off or pendulous, but fall away in a curve toward the throat. A wedge-shape head, or a head long and narrow in muzzle and back skull is incorrect as are massive, cheeky heads. The jaws are powerful and free from snippiness- the muzzle neither long and narrow nor short and stubby.

Nose- The nose should be wide and the nostrils well-developed. The nose should be black on black or yellow dogs, and brown on chocolates.

Nose color fading to a lighter shade is not a fault. A thoroughly pink nose or one lacking in any pigment is a disqualification.

Teeth- The teeth should be strong and regular with a scissors bite; the lower teeth just behind, but touching the inner side of the upper incisors. A level bite is acceptable, but not desirable. Undershot, overshot, or misaligned teeth are serious faults. Full dentition is preferred. Missing molars or pre-molars are serious faults.

Ears- The ears should hang moderately close to the head, set rather far back, and somewhat low on the skull; slightly above eye level. Ears should not be large and heavy, but in proportion with the skull and reach to the inside of the eye when pulled forward.

Eyes- Kind, friendly eyes imparting good temperament, intelligence and alertness are a hallmark of the breed. They should be of medium size, set well apart, and neither protruding nor deep set. Eye color should be brown in black and yellow Labradors, and brown or hazel in chocolates. Black, or yellow eyes give a harsh expression and are undesirable. Small eyes, set close together or round prominent eyes are not typical of the breed. Eye rims are black in black and yellow Labradors; and brown in chocolates. Eye rims without pigmentation is a disqualification.

Neck, Topline and Body: *Neck-* The neck should be of proper length to allow the dog to retrieve game easily. It should be muscular and free from throatiness. The neck should rise strongly from the shoulders with a moderate arch. A short, thick neck or a "ewe" neck is incorrect.

Topline- The back is strong and the topline is level from the withers to the croup when standing or moving. However, the loin should show evidence of flexibility for athletic endeavor.

Body- The Labrador should be short-coupled, with good spring of ribs tapering to a moderately wide chest. The Labrador should not be narrow chested; giving the appearance of hollowness between the front legs, nor should it have a wide spreading, bulldog-like front. Correct chest conformation will result in tapering between the front legs that allows unrestricted forelimb movement. Chest breadth that is either too wide or too narrow for efficient movement and stamina is incorrect. Slab-sided individuals are not typical of the breed; equally objectionable are rotund or barrel-chested specimens. The underline is almost straight, with little or no tuck-up in mature animals. Loins should be short, wide and strong; extending to well developed, powerful hindquarters. When viewed from the side, the Labrador Retriever shows a well-developed, but not exaggerated forechest.

Photo Courtesy of Kristin Daniello

CHAPTER 15 Showing

Tail- The tail is a distinguishing feature of the breed. It should be very thick at the base, gradually tapering toward the tip, of medium length, and extending no longer than to the hock. The tail should be free from feathering and clothed thickly all around with the Labrador's short, dense coat, thus having that peculiar rounded appearance that has been described as the "otter" tail. The tail should follow the topline in repose or when in motion. It may be carried gaily, but should not curl over the back. Extremely short tails or long thin tails are serious faults. The tail completes the balance of the Labrador by giving it a flowing line from the top of the head to the tip of the tail. Docking or otherwise altering the length or natural carriage of the tail is a disqualification.

Forequarters: Forequarters should be muscular, well-coordinated and balanced with the hindquarters.

Shoulders- The shoulders are well laid-back, long and sloping, forming an angle with the upper arm of approximately 90 degrees that permits the dog to move his forelegs in an easy manner with strong forward reach. Ideally, the length of the shoulder blade should equal the length of the upper arm. Straight shoulder blades, short upper arms or heavily muscled or loaded shoulders, all restricting free movement, are incorrect.

Front Legs- When viewed from the front, the legs should be straight with good strong bone. Too much bone is as undesirable as too little bone, and short legged, heavy boned individuals are not typical of the breed. Viewed from the side, the elbows should be directly under the withers, and the front legs should be perpendicular to the ground and well under the body. The elbows should be close to the ribs without looseness. Tied-in elbows or being "out at the elbows" interfere with free movement and are serious faults.

Pasterns should be strong and short and should slope slightly from the perpendicular line of the leg. Feet are strong and compact, with well-arched toes and well-developed pads. Dew claws may be removed. Splayed feet, hare feet, knuckling over, or feet turning in or out are serious faults.

Hindquarters: The Labrador's hindquarters are broad, muscular and well-developed from the hip to the hock with well-turned stifles and strong short hocks. Viewed from the rear, the hind legs are straight and parallel. Viewed from the side, the angulation of the rear legs is in balance with the front. The hind legs are strongly boned, muscled with moderate angulation at the stifle, and powerful, clearly defined thighs. The stifle is strong and there is no slippage of the patellae while in motion or when standing. The hock joints are strong, well let down and do not slip or hyper-extend while in motion or when standing. Angulation of both stifle and hock joint is such as to achieve the optimal balance of drive and traction. When standing the rear toes are only slightly behind the point of the rump. Over angulation produces a sloping topline not typical of the breed. Feet are strong and compact, with well-arched toes and well-developed pads. Cowhocks, spread hocks, sickle hocks and over-angulation are serious structural defects and are to be faulted.

Coat: The coat is a distinctive feature of the Labrador Retriever. It should be short, straight and very dense, giving a fairly hard feeling to the hand. The Labrador should have a soft, weather-resistant undercoat that provides protection from water, cold and all types of ground cover. A slight wave down the back is permissible. Woolly coats, soft silky coats, and sparse slick coats are not typical of the breed, and should be severely penalized.

Color: The Labrador Retriever coat colors are black, yellow and chocolate. Any other color or a combination of colors is a disqualification. A small white spot on the chest is permissible, but not desirable. White hairs from aging or scarring are not to be misinterpreted as brindling. ***Black-Blacks*** are all black. A black with brindle markings or a black with tan markings is a disqualification. ***Yellow-Yellows*** may range in color from fox-red to light cream, with variations in shading on the ears, back, and underparts of the dog. ***Chocolate-Chocolates*** can vary in shade from light to dark chocolate. Chocolate with brindle or tan markings is a disqualification.

Movement: Movement of the Labrador Retriever should be free and effortless. When watching a dog move toward oneself, there should be no sign of elbows out. Rather, the elbows should be held neatly to the body with the legs not too close together. Moving straight forward without pacing or weaving, the legs should form straight lines, with all parts moving in the same plane. Upon viewing the dog from the rear, one should have the impression that the hind legs move as nearly as possible in a parallel line with the front legs. The hocks should do their full share of the work, flexing well, giving the appearance of power and strength. When viewed from the side, the shoulders should move freely and effortlessly, and the foreleg should reach forward close to the ground with extension. A short, choppy movement or high knee action indicates a straight shoulder; paddling indicates long, weak pasterns; and a short, stilted rear gait indicates a straight rear assembly; all are serious faults. Movement faults interfering with performance including weaving; side-winding; crossing over; high knee action; paddling; and short, choppy movement, should be severely penalized.

Temperament: True Labrador Retriever temperament is as much a hallmark of the breed as the "otter" tail. The ideal disposition is one of a kindly, outgoing, tractable nature; eager to please and non-aggressive to-

CHAPTER 15   Showing

wards man or animal. The Labrador has much that appeals to people; his gentle ways, intelligence and adaptability make him an ideal dog. Aggressiveness towards humans or other animals, or any evidence of shyness in an adult should be severely penalized.

Disqualifications: *1. Any deviation from the height prescribed in the Standard. 2. A thoroughly pink nose or one lacking in any pigment. 3. Eye rims without pigment. 4. Docking or otherwise altering the length or natural carriage of the tail. 5. Any other color or a combination of colors other than black, yellow or chocolate as described in the Standard.*

After Selecting Your Puppy

When you pick up your puppy, the breeder will give you the Kennel Club registration document, so as soon as possible, you should change the registered ownership into your name, which you can do online. If you haven't owned a pedigree dog before, this is also a good time to fully acquaint yourself with the Kennel Club website, as it will be your go-to resource as you get into the world of showing.

You won't be able to show your dog until he is six months of age, but there is plenty of work to do over the coming months to begin getting your dog show ready. The first of these is socialization, as your dog is going to find himself in a busy environment, full of people and dogs, so he needs to be totally comfortable around both, as well as tolerate being handled by strangers.

As well as socializing your dog at puppy classes and in the park when he has completed his vaccinations, you can also take him out to visit dog shows close by. This will get him used to the hustle and bustle, so that the environment is totally familiar to him from the earliest age. You will also have the opportunity to observe all the show etiquette, and pick up tips. You may get to chat to experienced dog handlers, and watch how they "stack" their dog, which is the position your dog needs to be put into for judging. You can also learn to recognize the gait that a show champion needs when moving in the ring. Any contacts you are able to make in the showing world, especially fellow Labrador owners, will be valuable as you progress into the ranks with your dog.

Preparing for a Show

When you first get your Labrador puppy, register him with the Kennel Club in your country, and then it is a good idea to join the Labrador Retriever Club for your country also. These two organizations will be your guides through the world of top level showing.

If you only wish to show your dog for fun, then local shows are a great experience, where you can show off your Labrador Retriever, meet other owners and their dogs, and agree or disagree with the judge's decision, but always with good grace! Even if you want to compete in Kennel Club shows, local fun shows are a great place to start, as you and your dog can get used to the whole procedure in a low-pressure setting.

You need to plan ahead for the shows you wish to enter, by finding the show listings on the Kennel Club or Labrador Club website, or the local newspaper or local dog club website. Be sure to send your application and entry fee off in good time, then you can start planning for the big day.

If you are going to have to travel some distance to the show, you should also consider booking accommodation, so your dog can have time to settle before the event, especially if he suffers from travel sickness.

The Labrador Retriever requires very little grooming, and the judges are looking for a natural appearance. This means your dog should never be clipped, however his claws should be kept short through regular trimming that ensures the quick does not grow too long. The short coat of the Labrador Retriever cannot hide any faults, but in its natural glossy state will show off your dog's physical qualities to perfection. You should ensure through regular grooming that your dog has no scurf or flaking skin, and if you wish to bath your dog, this should be done a few days before the show, to enable the natural oils to return to the coat.

You should make cleaning your dog's teeth part of his regular routine from an early age, to ensure there is no tartar build-up, or worse – missing or decayed teeth, as these would constitute a fault in the show ring. You should also keep his ears clean.

If you have been attending shows as an observer, you will have seen how to stack your dog for the judge. And you will also have observed the kind of fluid gait in the ring that brings in the prizes. If you haven't actually had a chance to attend a show, there are plenty of videos online. These will help you know what to aim for, however they are no substitute for actually attending shows with your dog to get him familiar with the busy atmosphere.

CHAPTER 15 Showing

If you will be the one handling your dog in the ring, think about the outfit you will wear. This should be smart and comfortable, with practical shoes, so that you can move as effortlessly as your dog. The judge needs to see your dog's outline clearly against you, so if your Labrador is black or chocolate, you may consider wearing a lighter neutral color. Whereas if you have a yellow Labrador, wearing plain dark clothing will show him off to his best advantage.

You should not expect too much from your first show, as both you and your dog are getting used to it. Labradors are energetic by nature, and your dog may find the atmosphere hyper-stimulating, and resent keeping still to be judged, or moving gracefully at your heels. You shouldn't feel disappointed if you don't bring in the ribbons right away, or worse, feel that your dog has let you and himself down! You also should never question the judge's decision. Whereas your dog is being measured against the breed standard, there is inevitably some degree of personal preference in allocating the prizes. So, if it isn't your dog's day, there will always be another. And each event is a step on the way to showing your dog at his best!

CHAPTER 16
Living with a Senior Dog

Aging is an inevitable part of a dog's life, and preparing for it in advance is wise. A senior dog needs a different type of lifestyle from a young or adult dog, and this is especially true for Labradors. Labradors are prone to developing ailments which affect them later in life, such as arthritis, as discussed in Chapter 12.

Even though the life expectancy for a Labrador is 10-14 years old, you should start considering your Labrador a senior around the age of seven or eight. Subtle changes in his lifestyle at this stage will set him up for a long, happy and pain-free senior stage of his life, ensuring you can enjoy each other for longer. In this chapter, we will look at changes that will benefit your Labrador if implemented early, as well as how to deal with senior ailments, and what happens when the time comes to say goodbye.

Photo Courtesy of Nicole Justice

CHAPTER 16   Living with a Senior Dog

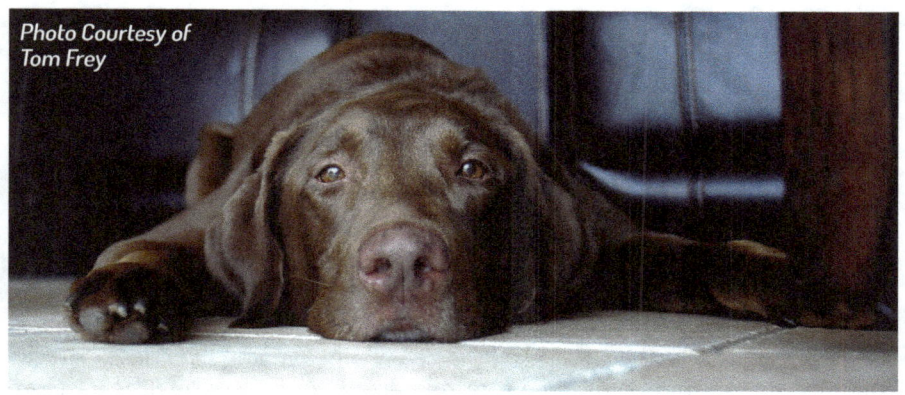

Photo Courtesy of Tom Frey

Diet

For a Labrador, diet is a huge topic which should not be overlooked. By the time the senior years roll in, most Labradors are overweight. This puts a major strain on your dog's heart, liver, kidneys and deteriorating joints. Unfortunately, an overweight Labrador is a common sight, so most people today do not realize that their Labrador is carrying some extra pounds. The best way to judge this is by looking back at the body condition scoring in Chapter 8, and aim for your Labrador to score a 4 or 5.

Switching to a senior dog diet will also help with your Labrador's weight. Senior dog diets are quite different from diets aimed at younger dogs as they are lower in calories and higher in fiber. This will help your Labrador feel full while still keeping the weight off him. The purpose of this is to match your dog's calorific requirements to his activity level, and in general, older dogs tend to exercise less.

Senior dog diets are also higher in omega oils. These are fatty acids which improve brain, heart, skin and eye health, as well as improve the lubrication of joints. In an aging body, omega oils can make a huge difference.

Sometimes, senior dog diets also have supplements incorporated into them, such as glucosamine and chondroitin. These help to maintain the cartilage of older, arthritic joints, and are discussed later in this chapter.

You don't need to change your Labrador over to a senior dog food as soon as he hits his seventh birthday, however before he is eight years old, it is worth aiming to have transitioned him onto it slowly. This is best done over the course of several weeks.

Senior Wellness Checks

> *Dogs' lives are too short. Their only fault, really.*
> **Agnes Sligh**

Your vet is highly valuable in your Labrador's senior years, and should not just be called upon when there is a problem. As highlighted in Chapter 11, preventative health care is so important, as prevention is always better than cure. This is where senior wellness checks come in, and should be made a routine part of your dog's healthcare from the age of eight and upward.

A senior wellness check is done once or twice a year, to ensure that your senior dog has not got any early signs of degenerative conditions. It will start with your veterinarian giving your Labrador a clinical examination. He will check your dog's teeth for tartar, and potentially recommend a dental procedure as discussed in Chapter 9 if they are dirty. He will also check your Labrador's eyes, ears, coat, heart, lungs, and abdomen. Finally, since Labradors are prone to developing arthritis later in life, your vet will carefully manipulate the dog's joints to feel for crepitus, which is a creaking sensation, and indicative of arthritis development.

After a full clinical examination, your vet might take a blood sample to check your Labrador's vital organs, such as kidneys and liver, and also might request a urine sample, as it will help with interpreting the results. A blood test can also pick up on early signs of certain cancers, as well as endocrine conditions and changes in the blood cells.

If there are any results which indicate that your dog's heart or kidneys are compromised, your vet is likely to also perform a blood pressure examination and possibly an ultrasound examination. However, these do not form the mainstay of a senior health check.

Finally, if your dog is on any chronic medication, this will be reviewed and the dose adjusted if needed.

By taking your Labrador for a senior health check once or twice yearly, you can rest assured that there is nothing underlying which hasn't been picked up and might be causing your Labrador ill health. Labradors are tough dogs, always wanting to please, and they often will hide signs of illness or discomfort in the early stages.

CHAPTER 16   Living with a Senior Dog

Advanced Arthritis

As discussed briefly in Chapter 12, arthritis usually stems from an underlying joint condition, such as trauma, joint dysplasia or osteochondrosis. But it can also be triggered by abnormal forces being placed on a normal joint, such as carrying extra weight or repetitive, strenuous exercise.

Arthritis is a degenerative disease of the whole joint. It is a common misunderstanding that it is a disease of the joint cartilage. In fact, the joint capsule, the subchondral bone under the cartilage, the joint fluid and the joint cartilage are all affected in different ways. As the joint degenerates, the cartilage becomes thinner, the subchondral bone cannot tolerate as much concussion, the joint fluid becomes thin and less in volume, and the joint capsule becomes inflamed. This all leads to a painful, non-functional joint.

The best way to manage arthritis is with multimodal management. That means just doing one thing is not going to help. If your Labrador doesn't have any underlying health conditions, your veterinarian can prescribe anti-inflammatories to help the joints. In addition to this, if your Labrador is carrying extra weight, this should immediately be addressed by putting him on a diet. Joint supplements can also aid in improving the joint, which include omega oils (to improve joint fluid viscosity and volume, as well as pro-

Photo Courtesy of Hanna Koskinen

vide natural anti-inflammatory effects) and glucosamine or chondroitin (to improve cartilage and joint fluid composition).

You might also want to consider complementary therapies to help your dog stay active. Veterinary physiotherapists can give you exercises to do at home, to keep your dog stretched and supple, as well as offer hydrotherapy which is a great way for your Lab to stay fit without extra strain being put on the joints. Specialist trained veterinarians can also perform acupuncture, which is an excellent pain-relieving modality without the need for drugs. Finally, CBD oil is becoming popular for controlling pain, however you need to be careful to buy an oil of high quality to make sure there is no psychogenic substance in it.

Dementia

Elderly dogs can develop a condition called "canine cognitive dysfunction," which is similar to dementia in humans. For short, it is known as CCD. This is a condition which cannot be prevented, nor can be treated, however there are some options to help improve your Labrador's quality of life if they do develop it.

Photo Courtesy of Carmel Wake

CCD causes a dulling of the brain. You might notice your old Labrador sleeping more than usual, looking dazed or confused, and have regressed in their potty training. The good news is that there is medication to improve the blood flow to the brain which helps to bring more oxygen to the brain cells. This allows them to work better and often gives senior dogs suffering with CCD a second lease of life.

Organ Deterioration

During the lifetime of any dog, the kidneys and liver are two organs which work extremely hard to filter out and remove waste products from the body. As a result, they can start to deteriorate in your dog's senior years. This is particularly evident in Labradors, as pain relief medications put an extra toll on the liver and kidneys, and since many Labradors have joint dysplasia or arthritis, chronic medication is common.

Symptoms may include loss of appetite, vomiting, drinking more and urinating more. In addition to this, liver disease may cause jaundice, which presents as yellow gums, and kidney disease may cause anemia, which presents as pale gums. Your veterinarian will assess the health of your Lab's internal organs through a blood test, and if he is concerned, may carry out an ultrasound examination.

There are excellent diets available for management of kidney disease and liver disease in older dogs, which is the main method of treatment. This reduces pressure on them to work hard to filter out waste products. In addition to that, there are medications available to help improve the efficiency of these organs, which a veterinarian will be able to dispense.

Anther organ which can show degenerative changes is the heart. The heart is a vital organ in the body. It pumps blood around to ensure all the cells receive oxygen and nutrients to be able to function. Sometimes, in older dogs, the valves inside the heart can become leaky. This can lead to some backflow and congestion. Symptoms include listlessness, fainting, coughing and getting out of breath easily. Starting heart medication early will reduce the pressure on the heart and significantly increase your dog's lifespan and prognosis.

Alongside the heart lie the lungs. Usually, the lung tissue is fairly elastic, which allows it to expand and contract as air is breathed in and out. An older dog's lungs become more fibrous with age, which means they don't expand as well. This is usually just an incidental condition that old dogs develop, and it doesn't affect them at all, but it can also lead to an inability to fight off infections. Therefore, older dogs are more likely to develop lung infections if exposed, in comparison to younger dogs.

Most senior dogs will develop some degree of organ degeneration in their senior years, but with senior health checks, this can be picked up quickly.

Loss of Senses

As well as the organs gradually deteriorating, a dog's senses can also be impacted by old age. Loss of the senses will not affect your dog medically or shorten his life-span, however, it may affect his quality of life to some degree.

The most common senses to deteriorate are hearing and sight. Luckily, it is very rare for a dog to lose their sense of smell, which is good as your Labrador is likely to love spending his walk with his nose to the ground, picking up all sorts of scents.

CHAPTER 16   Living with a Senior Dog

Surprisingly, dogs do extremely well without sight. If it happens suddenly, it may take your dog a while to adjust, however, if it is gradual, many owners do not even realize that their dogs have lost, or partially lost, their vision. The most common reasons why dogs lose their sight are cataracts and retinal atrophy, which are both discussed in Chapter 12. Most elderly dogs will develop nuclear sclerosis in their lenses, which can look like cataracts. But the cloudiness that it creates is not opaque, and your dog will be able to have some vision through it. If your Labrador begins to lose his sight, then teaching him to cope early on, is a good idea. As discussed previously, Labradors are exceptionally trainable. Teaching commands such as 'slowly', 'wait', 'turn' and 'stop' will prevent your dog from getting into trouble. He will also be able to navigate his way around the house with ease, as long as you keep the furniture in the same place, as his memory of navigating special areas will still be excellent.

Hearing loss, though, is slightly more difficult to manage. It is a good idea to prepare hearing loss at some point in your dog's life, and therefore when you teach him commands as a puppy, always combine a voice command with a signal. That way, if your dog loses some or all of his hearing, he can still understand you. Hearing loss is usually gradual though, and it is likely that you will not realize he is losing his hearing until it is quite far advanced. Unfortunately, there is nothing that can be done to regenerate your Labrador's hearing, but he can still live a happy life without it.

Bladder Control

Bladder control is something that many female dog owners may struggle with when their dogs become elderly. It is common for a spayed female to lose some control of her bladder, as estrogen plays a major role in tightening the sphincter at the exit of the bladder. Therefore, if the dog has not had many hormones during her life, then the bladder can possibly leak later on in life.

Another major cause of bladder leakage or loss of control is when the dog has arthritis in the lumbosacral area of the spine. Even though this is not a common site for Labradors to develop arthritis, they are still at a higher risk than other breeds. The nerves that come out of the spinal cord in this area are the ones which innervate the sphincter and bladder muscles. Compression of these nerves will lead to loss of control.

Determining the root cause of the loss of bladder control is essential when it comes to treatment. There are several medications available which help improve bladder control if it is due to lack of hormones, but if the reason is due to the back, then very little can be done. Doggy diapers are available to protect your home furnishings, and still allow your incontinent dog the freedom of the house.

It is important that if urine leaks excessively, then the area is bathed at least once daily to stop urine scald, and the hair is kept short in that area for hygiene reasons.

Saying Goodbye

Saying goodbye to your dog is never easy, and sometimes making the decision to put down your Labrador is not clear cut. Many degenerative conditions, such as arthritis and organ deterioration, are chronic in nature, and therefore some days will be good, and some will be bad. But in general, quality of life is what you should be monitoring, and when this deteriorates, this is an indicator that it is time.

This can be done through asking some basic questions:

1. Is your dog still happy and wagging his tail on a regular basis?
2. Is your dog still eager to eat? (which is obviously a big deal with a Labrador)
3. Does your dog still interact how he used to?
4. Can your dog still perform normal day to day activities?

If the answer to any of those is no, then his quality of life is compromised, and depending on the reason and prognosis, it may be the best option to consider euthanasia.

Euthanasia can seem like a sad topic, however, it should be seen as one last act of love that you can give your Labrador. Euthanasia is a way of being able to end suffering in a dignified manner. It is a peaceful procedure where an overdose of anesthetic is administered into a vein in the leg. It is non-painful and your Labrador will not feel any form of suffering. Some vets will give a dose of sedation before the procedure; however, it is not always necessary to make sure the procedure goes smoothly.

The injection can be done in the veterinary practice, but most vets will come to your home if you prefer your Labrador to stay in his own environment, which can be nice to reduce stress. There may be some muscle twitching after the injection, or a reflex which causes the dog to look like he is taking a deep breath, but these are natural things which happen after the

CHAPTER 16   Living with a Senior Dog

dog has passed away, so they are not indications that something has gone wrong. The veterinarian will confirm the passing by checking for a heartbeat with a stethoscope.

After your Labrador has passed away, your vet will be able to offer cremation services, either to have the ashes returned to you, or scattered in a pet crematorium, or you might wish to take your Labrador home for home burial.

Saying goodbye to your dog is really hard, even when it's expected and you know it's the right thing to do. However, this is the best time to think back about all the wonderful times you have had with your Labrador, and celebrate his life with all who have known him.

www.ingramcontent.com/pod-product-compliance
Lightning Source LLC
Chambersburg PA
CBHW062054280426
43661CB00087B/649